101 things you gotta do before you're 12!

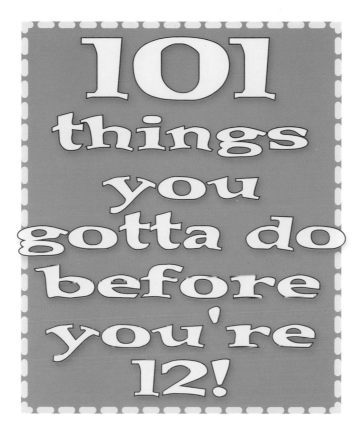

101 things you gotta do before you're 12!

Joanne O'Sullivan

LARK BOOKS

A Division of Sterling Publishing Co., Inc.
New York

Editor:
Joe Rhatigan

**Creative Director &
Cover Designer:**
Celia Naranjo

**Art Director &
Photo Researcher:**
Ginger Graziano

Assistant Editor:
Rose McLarney

**Art Production
Assistant:**
Bradley Norris

Cover Photography:
Clockwise from upper left: ©Lynne
Siler Photography; ©Photo Resource
Hawaii/Alamy; © Lynne Siler
Photography; ©Anna Peislzefa/Corbis;
©Michael Pole/Corbis; ©Brian A.
Vikander/Corbis; ©Shutterstock/
James G. Mcconnell

10 9 8 7 6 5 4 3 2 1

First Edition

Published by Lark Books, A Division of
Sterling Publishing Co., Inc.
387 Park Avenue South, New York, N.Y. 10016

Distributed in Canada by Sterling Publishing, c/o Canadian Manda Group, 165 Dufferin Street,
Toronto, Ontario, Canada M6K 3H6

Distributed in the United Kingdom by GMC Distribution Services, Castle Place, 166 High Street, Lewes,
East Sussex, England BN7 1XU

Distributed in Australia by Capricorn Link (Australia) Pty Ltd., P.O. Box 704, Windsor, NSW 2756 Australia

If you have questions or comments about this book, please contact:
Lark Books, 67 Broadway, Asheville, NC 28801
(828) 253-0467

Manufactured in China

ISBN 13: 978-1-57990-859-1
ISBN 10: 1-57990-859-4

For information about custom editions, special sales, and premium and corporate purchases,
please contact Sterling Special Sales Department at 800-805-5489 or specialsales@sterlingpub.com.

Contents

Introduction

You probably have a lot of to-do lists in your life to remind you about important things: doing your homework, feeding your pet, or keeping up with your chores, to name a few. But there are lots of things worth remembering that you might *not* have a list for. With your busy school and activity schedule, you might forget to have adventures, like going on a whale watch or finding your way through a corn maze. You might not remember to try new things, like celebrating a holiday you usually don't celebrate or eating a flower. And it may never even cross your mind to do something a little wacky, like entering a sandcastle-making competition or taking part in a mud run. This book is here to remind you to do a lot of fun, exciting, amusing, and amazing things that you might otherwise overlook (and you'd really hate missing out on). Between walking the dog and getting your science project done, make some room for the experiences on this very different kind of to-do list. You won't get paid any allowance or get a grade for completing them, but you'll have some incredible, challenging, and way cool experiences.

How to Use This Book

Read through all the 101 entries in the book—figure out which things you've already done and which things you really want to do next. Some things you can do any time you like, while others require planning, and still others can only be done at specific times (seeing a meteor shower or an eclipse, for example). You'll be able to do many things all on your own, but for others, you'll have more fun with a friend, and some will call for your parents to be involved. While many entries are for one-time-only experiences, there are many that are ongoing: earning and saving money, for example, happen over time, and making the world a better place is one of those things you'll still be trying to do long after your 12th birthday.

Get out there and start doing! You don't have to do the list in order—pick whatever sounds good to you at the moment. Challenge yourself to do as many different things as you can, and don't give up if you can't get something done on your first try (chances are, you've still got plenty of time left to finish it before you turn 12). Congratulate yourself when you check another entry off your list!

Use the **stickers** to keep track of what you've done and what you want to do next. You can make a Top 20 list so that you're sure to do things that are most important to you. Use the stickers to rank your experiences. Each entry has a **hand symbol** to show you where to put your sticker (but you can, of course, put it wherever you like).

Keep this book handy. When you're bored, restless, or can't think of anything fun to do, take it out, and tackle a new entry. Use it as inspiration for creating a lifelong to-do list.

Most of all, don't let the list become just another bunch of things you *have to* do: **stop at once if you're not having fun!** It's all about exploring the world, learning new things, and having a great time while you're doing it, and that is really the best part about being younger than 12!

1 Celebrate a Holiday you Usually Don't Celebrate

To find out more about holidays in specific months or countries, go to www.earthcalandar.net

Almost every day is a holiday somewhere in the world, so there are always a lot of good excuses to celebrate. The dates people observe and their customs for doing so can teach you a lot about another culture—you can try new food, learn new games, and have a whole different kind of fun. If you live in a city with a large immigrant population, you can easily find events marking different holidays. Chinese New Year celebrations are held in cities all over the world, and so are fiestas celebrating the Mexican holiday Cinco de Mayo (May 5). Carnival or Mardi Gras parades and festivities happen every winter and Diwali; the Hindu Festival of Lights comes around each fall. If you don't live somewhere where there's a public celebration, make your own party. Host a bonfire for the Scandinavian holiday Midsummer's Eve or make a Korean meal for Chuseok, Korean thanksgiving. So many holidays, so much fun to be had.

Something to Celebrate

There's something to celebrate every month. Here are some ideas to get you started:

JANUARY

January 6 —Twelfth Night, Epiphany, or Three Kings' Day The last of the "twelve days of Christmas," this holiday is celebrated in many European and Latin American countries.

FEBRUARY

Date changes yearly—Mardi Gras Day or Fat Tuesday Celebrated with parades and costume balls in Europe, French Canada, and on the Gulf Coast of the United States.

MARCH

Date changes yearly (sometimes in January or February)—Chinese New Year Celebrated in Chinese communities around the world with fireworks, colorful parades, and feasts.

APRIL

April 13–15—Songkran, Thai New Year Celebrated by "water splashing," house cleaning, and other rituals.

MAY

May 1—May Day or Beltane This day marks the coming of spring in many countries, especially in Europe. Celebrated with the creation of a maypole and the crowning of a May Queen.

May 5—Cinco de Mayo
Honors a Mexican battle victory; celebrated in many Mexican communities with parades, traditional dancing, and feasts.

JUNE

June 24—Midsummer Eve and Midsummer Day Celebrated in Scandinavia with bonfire parties, dancing, singing, and flower picking.

Date changes yearly—Chinese Dragon Boat Festival Honoring a Chinese poet, this holiday is celebrated in Chinese communities everywhere with dragon-boat races.

JULY

July 14—Bastille Day (French Independence Day) Celebrated by French people around the world with fireworks, street parties, and picnics.

AUGUST

Date changes yearly—O-bon Ancestor remembrance day in Japan; celebrated with family reunions, cleaning graves, drumming, and dancing.

SEPTEMBER

Date changes yearly—Chuseok (Korean thanksgiving) Harvest festival celebrated with feasts and ancestor-remembrance rituals.

Date changes yearly—Diwali (Festival of Lights) This Indian holiday is celebrated with lamps, fireworks, marigold wreaths, and gift giving.

Date changes yearly—Ulambana (Festival of Hungry Ghosts) In Asia and Southeast Asia, this holiday is celebrated with feasts, bonfires, and tributes to ward off bad spirits.

NOVEMBER

November 2—El Día de los Muertos (The Day of the Dead) Mexican ancestor-remembrance holiday; celebrated with the creation of altars and picnics in cemeteries.

DECEMBER

December 26—Boxing Day Celebrated in England and former British colonies, this is a day to make charitable contributions.

2 Join (or Start) a Club or Team

You might think you're the only one in your school or town who loves _____ (chess, ballroom dancing, racquetball, mystery novels—fill in the blank with your favorite activity or hobby). But with just a little checking around, you may be surprised to find out just how many others share your interest—enough to form a club, in fact. There may be an existing group nearby, but if there's not, you can always organize one yourself. Put out the word at school and like-minded enthusiasts will come to you. The point of a club or team is not to be exclusive or keep others out; it's to enjoy your shared activity together, learn from each other, and maybe make some new friends. Your club might even compete with other clubs or take part in bigger events, such as conventions. Join up, start up, or sign up—there's strength in numbers, and it's good to be part of something bigger than just you.

3 GO TO A DEMONSTRATION, PROTEST, OR RALLY

When you're a little kid, you might not know much about what's going on in the world or even in your own town. But as you get older, you discover that there are a lot of "issues." Everyone has his or her own opinion about an issue, and you're expected to have one, too. When an issue is really "hot," people are bound to hold a rally, protest, or demonstration to drum up support for their opinion. At a rally, people give speeches and sing or chant. Sometimes things may get a little tense—people might start to shout and argue with those who *don't* agree with them, and it can be kind of uncomfortable to watch. But it's still a great way to learn about what people think and why. Go to demonstrations for more than one side of an issue and make up your own mind.

sleep under the stars

You may have those glow-in-the-dark stars on your bedroom ceiling at home: that doesn't count. For a truly amazing, unforgettable experience you've gotta actually sleep *outside* under the stars in a sleeping bag (or even in a tent). Under a great big sky, you think great big thoughts—how big is the universe? Are we alone in it, or could there be another planet out there similar to ours? It's not the stuff you normally think about, but that's why it's worth doing. You don't have to be out in the wilderness to sleep under the stars (although you can see way more stars that way). Even some famously urban places like Dodger Stadium in Los Angeles or the New York City Parks Department invite kids to camp out on special occasions. Try it some time and see if you can unlock any of the mysteries of the universe before you go to sleep.

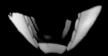

Scan the Skies

Before you fall asleep under the stars, look for Polaris, also called the North Star. Used for centuries by navigators as the indicator of "true north," it's said to be the brightest star in the sky. Because it's very close to the Earth's rotational axis, it appears never to move, and the other stars appear to revolve around it. To find it, locate the Little Dipper—it's the last star in the Dipper's "handle."

5 Walk a Maze or Labyrinth

You may have put together a puzzle before, but have you ever walked one? A maze is an age-old, life-size puzzle designed to put your brain *and* your feet to the test. You enter a single path but must quickly choose from among many different routes, some leading to dead ends, others leading farther in, and one eventually leading out of the maze. Which do you choose? How do you decide? Your sense of direction and logic are your only guides. There are garden hedge mazes, and corn or maize mazes cut into corn fields in the late summer and early fall. A turf maze or labyrinth is another kind of walkable path. Instead of getting you lost, walking a labyrinth is said to bring you inner peace. There are no dead ends in a labyrinth—just a single twisting, turning path that leads you to the center. Whether you choose to walk a maze or a labyrinth, you'll be following in the footsteps of countless generations, and you'll emerge a tad wiser than when you started.

6 Go to a Powwow

Chances are, most of what you know about Native American culture comes from books and movies. Going to a powwow gives you the opportunity to experience the real culture in real life. A powwow is a gathering that's part serious, part fun, and full of meaning. Powwows bring together Native American communities for a chance to celebrate and pass on traditions to new generations, but everyone is invited to attend. Each ceremony has different activities, but most include singing, dancing, and drumming contests, all performed in amazing ceremonial regalia. The rhythms of the songs, pounding of the drums, and the swirling colors of the outfits all combine to make an experience you'll never forget.

For more information on where you can find a powwow in the United States or Canada, check out the calendars at www.powwows.com or www.500nations.com /500_Powwows .asp.

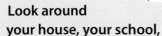

Look around
your house, your school,
your community—you probably have an old
bike in need of repair, an overgrown city park near your house, even
an unused and gloomy part of your basement—they *could* be great—
all they need is a little love. Pick your project and figure out what
you need to do make it work. You may need to enlist friends or your
parents to help. Spread your enthusiasm and help them to see what
you see—a lot of potential just waiting to be discovered.

FIX A BIKE AND MAKE IT YOUR OWN

Wouldn't it be great if you got something free at the end of every class you took? Many communities or local bike stores offer programs that teach you how to repair an old bike, and then let you keep it! Check with your local parks and recreation department, or do an Internet search with the words "earn a bike," "community bike," "bike recycling," "bike library," or "bike co-op."

You can also find programs in your area by looking at www.ibike.org/ encouragement/ youth-directory. htm.

8 CONQUER A FEAR

Although some of your friends may *claim* to be fearless, *everyone* is afraid of *something*. It could be a little thing, *really little*, such as small, creepy crawly bugs or a big thing like "the dark." Most people are afraid of a little of each type. There are definitely things that are good to be afraid of—wild animals with big teeth, for example. But there are other fears that get in your way: being afraid of the diving board can keep you from joining the swim team, and being afraid of speaking in public can keep you from running for class officer. The best way to tackle them is bit by bit. You don't have to jump off the high dive right away or speak in front of the whole school. Work up to the low board, taking your time; give a speech to your stuffed animals. Once you get comfortable, you can take the next steps. You may never *love* your former fear, but at least you can stop it from getting in your way.

To find a rail-trail near you, go to www.railtrails.org.

There are 1,396 rail-trails in the U.S. alone, totaling 13,361 in rail-trail miles. 1,200 more trails are in the making.

9 Ride, Hike, or Walk a Rail-Trail

They call it one of the biggest recycling projects in history—turning old, out-of-use railroad tracks into pathways for hiking, biking, walking, skiing, skating, or even horseback riding. Where steam trains once trundled coal, freight, or mail down the tracks, hikers and bikers now trek through tunnels and ride over railroad trestles. Rail-trails take you past some of the most amazing scenery you'll see anywhere—from the rugged peaks of the Rockies on Colorado's Galloping Goose Trail to the rocky Pacific coast on the Monterey Peninsula Recreational Trail. There are short trails in cities, long trails through the country-side or even through the desert—each one is a different kind of adventure. You'll see what train passengers of old used to see, no ticket required.

10 CARE FOR A PET

They're cute and cuddly, swift and slippery, fluffy and feathery. A pet is more than just another thing to play with—it becomes a living, breathing member of your family. But it's not always easy to care for a pet. The bigger the pet, the more work it is to care for. A horse *sounds* great, but it needs a lot of food, exercise, and cleanup, not to mention space, time, and money. So which pet is right for you? Cats and dogs are the most common choices; birds, hamsters, gerbils, and guinea pigs are a little more low maintenance and will fit easily in your house, no matter their size. Fish and rabbits make good pets, or you might go even more exotic with a gecko, iguana, or snake. Promise to take good care of your pet, and you'll have a new pal from a different species.

11
Walk a Swinging Bridge

Your parents would *never* let you go bungee jumping—and besides it's pretty much against the law until you're 14. But if your inner thrill-seeker can't wait that long, why not try bungee walking? That's what some call walking across a swinging footbridge stretching over a river or gorge. It's the kind of bridge that, in action movies like *Indiana Jones*, snaps when someone is halfway across, leaving him dangling from a fraying cord, hundreds of feet off the ground. Don't worry—in real life, they're very safe, but it's still pretty adventurous to cross one. Beneath your feet, the bridge sways and creaks loudly—you'll be convinced that this is the moment that it's going down. Just keep walking and don't look down, until you get to the other side! When you get there you may just feel brave enough to turn around and do it again.

Where to Find Swinging Bridges

Buffalo, New York
In Cazenovia Park, designed by architect Fredrick Law Olmstead

Delphi, Indiana
Crosses Deer Creek in Riley Park, named for the poet James Whitcomb Riley

York, Maine
The "Wiggly Bridge," leading to Stedman Woods Nature Preserve, may be the world's smallest suspension bridge.

Greenville, South Carolina
In Reedy Park, with nearby restaurants and shopping

San Jose, California
Crosses the Guadalupe River in Guadalupe River Park

Thermopolis, Wyoming
Crosses Muddy River, in Lava Canyon Park near Mt. Saint Helens

Toronto, Canada
Bridge to CN Tower and the Skydome

Find maps and information about these and many other bridges around the world by visiting www.waymarking.com and searching for "suspension bridges."

SEE A METEOR SHOWER

An old superstition says that if you see a shooting star, you'll have good luck. If that's the case, seeing as many as 50 of them in one night—possible only during a meteor shower—will set you up with good luck for life. Even if it doesn't lead to good luck, a meteor shower is certainly a good show. This sky-high spectacle happens when the Earth passes through the path of debris from a comet. The debris burns through Earth's upper atmosphere, creating brilliant streaks of light that look like shooting stars. To see the out-of-this-world sight, you'll need to be in the right place at the right time: a dark spot, away from bright city lights, between midnight and daybreak on particular days of the year (see opposite page). Fix your eyes in the right position on the horizon and you'll see one of the night sky's greatest displays—if you're lucky.

NIGHTS OF THE SHOOTING STARS

Meteor showers happen around the same time every year. They're named after the constellations in which they appear. The dates of the showers change slightly every year, but here's a guide to go by. For a yearly meteor shower calendar, go to www.stardate.org and type "meteor showers" in the search box.

Quadrantids	early January
Lyrids	April
Eta Aquarids	May
Delta Aquarids	late July
Alpha Capricornids	late July, early August
Perseids	mid-August
Orionids	mid- to late October
South Taurids	early November
North Taurids	early November
Leonids	mid-November
Geminids	mid-December
Ursids	late December

HOW TO SEE METEOR SHOWERS

Your eyes are all you need to see a meteor shower. No telescope or binoculars are required. But these tips will help.

◆ Ask an adult to go outside with you between midnight and dawn.

◆ Find a dark place. Get away from the city and car headlights. Allow your eyes to adjust for 15 minutes. Can you see the stars well enough to pick out constellations? Then it's dark enough.

◆ Bring blankets or chairs. Snacks improve stargazing.

◆ Watch the sky. When you see lots of shooting stars streaking out of one point, called the radiant, that's a meteor shower.

◆ If you look to the side of the meteor shower instead of directly at the radiant, you can see it better.

13 SEE A GREAT RACE

READY, SET, GO!

Here are some of the biggest races in North America, on two legs, two wheels, four legs, or a sled:

BIKE RACES

Tour de Georgia
When: Every April
Where: Throughout the state
Why: It's the only Class 2 pro bike race in North America

USPro Championship
When: Every June
Where: Philadelphia, PA
Why: Largest single-day pro cycling event in the United States

MARATHONS

New York City Marathon
When: Every November
Where: The five boroughs of New York City
Why: The most famous U.S. marathon

Boston Marathon
When: Every April
Where: Downtown Boston, MA
Why: The world's oldest annual marathon

Chicago Marathon
When: Every October
Where: Downtown Chicago, IL
Why: One of the largest marathons in the United States

Ironman Triathlon
When: Every August (BC) and October (Hawaii)

And they're off! There's a sense of excitement in the air right as a race begins—at that moment, anything is possible, and anyone could emerge as the winner. But watching any part of a great race is fun—you can cheer on your favorite, or just cheer on everyone who's giving it a try. What makes a race a great one? Great competitors and a long history are a start. A marathon is cool to watch, but there's something about watching the New York or Boston marathons that makes you feel like you're part of something big. It may even inspire you to start training for a marathon of your own.

Where: Penticton, BC, and Kailua-Kona, HI
Why: Running, swimming, biking all in one race

HORSE RACES

The Kentucky Derby
When: First Sunday in May
Where: Louisville, KY
Why: The most famous horse race in the United States

Belmont Stakes
When: Every June
Where: Elkmont, NY
Why: Part of the "triple crown" of horse racing

DOGSLED RACES

The Iditarod
When: Every March
Where: Over 1,150 miles, Anchorage to Nome, AK
Why: One of the toughest races in the world

Upper Peninsula 200, Midnight Run, and Jack Pine 30 Races
When: Every February
Where: Marquette, MI
Why: Chance to see a dogsled race in the Lower 48

Sure, there may be faster ways and more convenient ways to travel these days, but taking a train is more about the journey than getting to the destination, especially if you take an old-fashioned steam train. The whistle blows, and you know you're off on an adventure. There's something exciting about the train's motion and rhythm on the track, and the way the city or countryside rolls by you. You can see things that you'd never see from a car, stretch out and walk around much more than you could in a plane, and even enjoy a meal in the dining car. If you take an overnight train journey, you get to experience the fun pull-down beds and sinks in the sleeping compartment. Even your local commuter train or the subway can be fun—take it to the end of the line one time and see where you end up.

15 Have a Lazy Saturday

Homework, practices, rehearsals, and volunteer work—most kids today find themselves pretty busy every day of the week. "Overscheduled" is how most parents describe it. It's good to be busy, but it's also good to slow down every once in a while. Try to keep one Saturday open every month or so—no sleepovers, no games, and nowhere to be when you first wake up in the morning. At first, this might sound suspiciously like something you've been trying to avoid: *boredom*. But don't freak out and try to fill up your day. Let the day take you along; go with the flow. Think of all the places you've wanted to go and things you've wanted to do but haven't had time for... now might be the perfect day. Or just *really* be lazy: hang out in a hammock, lie in the grass and watch the clouds go by, play Frisbee with your dog. Whatever you do, don't put too much effort into it; you can go back to your busy schedule tomorrow.

29

16 READ A CLASSIC

Many kids think that, when it refers to a book, the word *classic* is just a code word for "boring." Visions of really heavy books with lots of pages, old-fashioned language, not much action, and characters you wouldn't want to eat lunch with may come to mind. But just because your librarian tells you a certain book is a classic is no reason to avoid it. There are a lot of classics that are classic for a good reason: they're really great reads. They may take you to faraway places or imaginary worlds. They have characters that you can relate to, even though they may have lived hundreds of years ago. They have mystery, danger, and drama, and it's not even against the rules for classics to be funny. And besides, saying you've read a few classics makes you sound really smart.

COOL CLASSICS (GUARANTEED!)

Alexander, Lloyd. *Prydain Chronicles*
Babbitt, Natalie. *Tuck Everlasting*
Baum, L. Frank. *The Wonderful Wizard of Oz*
Boston, L. M. *The Children of Green Knowe*
Brink, Carol Ryrie. *Caddie Woodlawn*
Burnett, Frances Hodgson. *The Secret Garden*
Byars, Betsy. *The Summer of the Swans*
Cooper, Susan. *The Dark is Rising Sequence*
Dodge, Mary Mapes. *Hans Brinker, or the Silver Skates*
Eager, Edward. *Half Magic*
Edmonds, Walter D. *The Matchlock Gun*
Enright, Elizabeth. *Thimble Summer*
Estes, Eleanor. *The Moffats*
Farley, Walter. *The Black Stallion*
Field, Rachel. *Hitty: Her First Hundred Years*
Fitzhugh, Louise. *Harriet the Spy*
Gardiner, John Reynolds. *Stone Fox*
George, Jean Craighead. *My Side of the Mountain*
Grahame, Kenneth. *The Wind in the Willows*
Grimm, Jacob and Wilhelm. *Grimm's Complete Fairy Tales*
Henry, Marguerite. *Misty of Chincoteague*
Howe, Deborah. *Bunnicula*
Hughes, Langston. *The Dream Keeper and Other Poems*
Irving, Washington. *Rip Van Winkle*
Juster, Norton. *The Phantom Tollbooth*
Kipling, Rudyard. *The Jungle Books*

Knight, Eric. *Lassie Come Home*
Konigsburg, E. L. *From the Mixed-up Files of Mrs. Basil E. Frankweiler*
Lamb, Charles and Mary. *Tales from Shakespeare*
Lenski, Lois. *Strawberry Girl*
Lewis, C. S. *The Chronicles of Narnia*
Lindgren, Astrid. *Pippi Longstocking*
Lofting, Hugh. *Doctor Dolittle*
Lovelace, Maud Hart. *Betsy-Tacy*
Macaulay, David. *Castle*
Montgomery, L. M. *Anne of Green Gables*
Nesbit, E. *The Railway Children*
North, Sterling. *Rascal*
Norton, Mary. *The Borrowers*
O'Brien, Robert C. *Mrs. Frisby and the Rats of Nimh*
Paterson, Katherine. *Bridge to Terabithia*
Pearce, Philippa. *Tom's Midnight Garden*
Sewell, Anna. *Black Beauty*
Sharp, Margery. *The Rescuers*
Speare, Elizabeth George. *The Witch of Blackbird Pond*
Spyri, Johanna. *Heidi*
Travers, P. L. *Mary Poppins*
Wilder, Laura Ingalls. *Little House on the Prairie*
Wyss, Johann D. *The Swiss Family Robinson*

17
FLOAT A LAZY RIVER

Steaming hot day—no breeze, no clouds in the sky, no relief. What do you do to beat the heat? Spend the whole day on a deliciously cool river. Pack lots of snacks and icy cold beverages in a cooler, put on your sunscreen and life vest, and rent an inner tube or a raft to get you out on the water. Bring your friends and tie your tubes together for a flotilla of fun. Forget paddling (unless you get stuck). Once you're in, let the current take you at its own pace—the slower, the better. Depending on the river you choose, it could take you from two to six hours to float all the way from your "put in" to your "take out" point. Drape your arms and legs over the sides and let them soak. It's the true meaning of "chilling out."

Learn Some Self-Defense

Hopefully, you'll never have to use it, but just in case, it's good to know a few strategies for protecting yourself. The first and best thing you can learn is how to keep yourself from risk in the first place by avoiding dangerous situations. Your school, scout troop, or local police department probably offers classes or workshops that will give you lots of tips and practical advice. You don't need to have a black belt in karate or another martial art to be safe. Even if you're small and not very strong, there are moves you can learn that can give you an advantage, or just a few minutes to get away. A combination of awareness, quick thinking, and some self-defense tactics will help you be prepared and stay safe.

19 | MAKE A TIME CAPSULE

Where will you be in five years? How about 10 years? Will you remember how things are today after so much time has passed? Why not create a record of your life right now to make sure you don't forget? Making a time capsule is a fun project that will help you document the way things are for you right here, right now, so that your memories won't be lost over time. Create the time capsule by yourself or with your friends or family. Years from now, it will be fun to look back and compare what's different and the same about the world and about *you*. If you bury the time capsule or conceal it outside, be sure to keep the instructions on how to find it—otherwise, some kid 100 years from now might be the next one to open it.

HOW TO MAKE A TIME CAPSULE

CHOOSE a container for your time capsule—anything from a plastic container with a lid to a shoebox will do (an airtight metal container is best if it will be stored underground).

FILL the container with items that represent you and your life at this moment in time. Make a list of your favorites, including your favorite song, book, actor or actress, color, TV show, movie, food, place, etc. Sign and date the list.

INCLUDE pictures of yourself, your room, your pets, your family, and your friends. Write a brief description of the subject on the back of each photo. School schedules or copies of recent reports or papers you've written will also be interesting to look at in a few years.

INCLUDE ticket stubs from movies or events you've been to recently and a copy of the local newspaper to show the date. This gives the future you an idea of what was going on in the world, how much things cost, etc., at the time you made the capsule.

WRITE a letter to yourself in the future saying what's on your mind right now. Give predictions about what your life will be like at the time you open the capsule. It will be fun to find out whether your predictions come true!

DECIDE on a time to open the time capsule—from one year to five years from now, or any time in between. Finally, decide on a place to hide the time capsule, seal your container tightly, and put it away, making sure you leave a note somewhere to pinpoint its exact location.

20 See a Famous, Outrageous Parade

It's not every day that you get to see pirates walking down the middle of the street or hundreds of mermaids swishing their way by. You almost never get to see dozens of cars rolling along, decorated like sharks or dragons, or have people on stilts throw candy and necklaces at you. That's why going to a parade where one of these rare and wonderful scenes takes place is a must. Ordinary parades can be fun— you've got your marching bands, your local beauty queens, your clown patrol. But some parades go out of their way to be over the top. At a Mardi Gras parade, you compete with others for beads thrown from the floats. At the annual Mermaid Parade in Coney Island, New York, everyone is a mermaid, and pirates rule at the Gasparilla Children's Parade, held every year in Tampa, Florida. Check with your local tourism office to see whether there's a famous or famously outrageous parade near you.

21 PLAN A DREAM TRIP

The Taj Mahal, the pyramids, the Eiffel Tower, Machu Picchu… you'll get there some day. Anything is possible with planning. The first step is to gather as much information as you can about your dream destination. Research the currency and the exchange rate, the transportation situation (how will you get there and how long will it take), and the weather at different times of year so you'll know the best time to go. Find out about any health or safety issues: Will you need any vaccines? Is the country experiencing a civil war or an upswing in crime? (Might want to rethink that place…) Next, figure out a budget. How much would it cost to go there? Calculate your figures based on different options, such as the time of year you go, the kind of place you stay in, and how long you stay. Once you've got it all figured out, propose the trip to your parents… if it doesn't work out now, don't worry. The whole world is out there waiting for you.

22 Run (or Play) in the Mud

Running, sliding, diving through the mud, getting dirtier than you ever imagined, and knowing that not only will you not get in trouble for it, but you might actually win a medal! It sounds too good to be true, but there are actually competitions called mud runs that let you do just that. The first mud run was created by the U.S. Marines, who actually run through muddy obstacle courses as part of their training. Now you can watch (or even participate in) mud runs all over the place—maybe even in your hometown. If not, organize your own mud run in your yard or in a park. Pick a really muddy spot (or muddy it up with a garden hose), create an obstacle course (things to go over, under, or around), and decide on a finish line. Invite your friends to join you. You'll have so much fun on the course that you may forget you're competing. Just be sure to hose off before you go inside.

Some Famous Mud Runs

Kid's Mud Run Canada
When: **Check website**
Where: **Toronto, ON**
www.mudrun.ca

ASYMCA Mini-Mud Run
When: **Check website**
Where: **Norfolk, VA**
www.asymcamudrun.com

Marine Mud Run Polywog Jog (kid's race)
When: **Every September**
Where: **Roanoke, VA**
www.mudrun.com

World Famous Mud Run (adults only; kids can watch)
When: **Every June**
Where: **Camp Pendleton, CA**
www.camppendletonraces.com

San Diego Mud Run (Youth 1k Mini-Mud Run)
When: **Check website**
Where: **San Diego, CA**
www.sandiegomudrun.com

Bivalve Bash Kid's Mud Run
When: **Check website**
Where: **Taylor Shellfish Farms, Bow, WA**
www.taylorshellfishfarms.com

23 Go to the Fair

It's pretty safe to say that there's only one place where you can find pigs, goats, bunnies, llamas, pie-eating contests, prize-winning pumpkins and pickles, Ferris wheels, and fried Twinkies all at the same time—it's at a fair. In the past, the fair (often called the agricultural, county, or state fair) was *the* big event of the year in rural communities, and in many it still is (the State Fair of Texas features more than 50 rides and 8,000 animals, and it draws more than 100,000 visitors each year). Kids can compete in lots of events, from a chili cook-off to butter sculpting to a livestock show, or just have fun at the arcades or on the carnival rides. Each fair reflects the culture of the area where it's held, so each is unique. Fairs are an end-of-summer or a fall thing, and most are held in rural areas, but you can find them even near big cities. Check one out for food, fun, and farm animals.

To find a water trail in your state or province, check the American Canoe Association's directory at www.acanet.org/recreation/watertrails.lasso.

24 Hit the (Water) Trail

When you hear the word *trail*, you probably think of a path through the woods—a place you travel with boots on your feet and a pack on your back. But have you ever heard of a water trail? Same idea, except you've got a paddle in your hand and a canoe or kayak underneath you. Water trails were the first North American "highways." Long before there were roads cutting through the wilderness, explorers charted the continent from their canoes. There are water trails in lakes, rivers, and even the ocean. Like hiking trails, they can be long or short, for beginners or experts, and there are signs and maps to keep you from getting lost. Lewis and Clark, Samuel de Champlain, Jacques Cartier—all the famous *voyageurs* saw North America by canoe or kayak—shouldn't you?

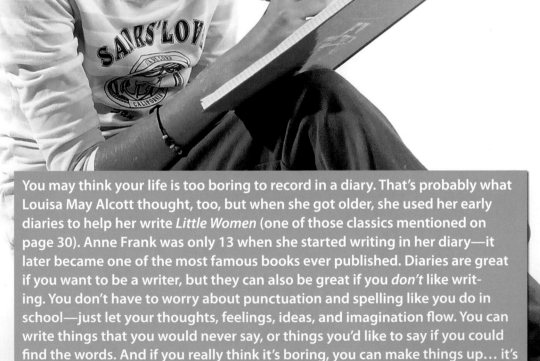

25

Start a Journal or Diary

You may think your life is too boring to record in a diary. That's probably what Louisa May Alcott thought, too, but when she got older, she used her early diaries to help her write *Little Women* (one of those classics mentioned on page 30). Anne Frank was only 13 when she started writing in her diary—it later became one of the most famous books ever published. Diaries are great if you want to be a writer, but they can also be great if you *don't* like writing. You don't have to worry about punctuation and spelling like you do in school—just let your thoughts, feelings, ideas, and imagination flow. You can write things that you would never say, or things you'd like to say if you could find the words. And if you really think it's boring, you can make things up… it's your journal, so there are no rules.

Dear Diary

SOME FAMOUS KIDS' JOURNALS

Louisa May Alcott

She began writing in her diary at age seven and recorded events that inspired the novel *Little Women*.

Beatrix Potter

The author of *Peter Rabbit* kept her diary in code.

Theodore Roosevelt

His journal provides a look at the future president when he was 10 and asthmatic—and made spelling errors.

Anne Frank

This 13-year-old kept her now-famous diary as she and her family hid from the Nazis in an attic for two years.

Zlata Filipovic

This 11-year-old Bosnian's diary changed dramatically when civil war began in her country. "I am not writing to you about me anymore. I'm writing to you about war, death, injuries, shells, sadness, and sorrow," she wrote.

Helena Morley

This 12-year-old Brazilian girl kept a diary and thought she was recording only daily, small-town life. But the important poet Elizabeth Bishop loved the diary and translated it.

How to Start Your Own

FREEWRITING

Write something. Write anything. Don't stop writing until you fill up a page. Don't even lift the pen from the paper. Then, go back and read what you wrote. Freewriting is not supposed to be good writing. But are there ideas in your free writing that you could turn into something more?

LISTS

Making lists will help you quickly organize and focus your thoughts. And you don't have to use complete sentences.

LETTERS

Compose letters that you'll never send. Your journal is a private vault for all your great/weird/horrible ideas.

A bus tour, a carriage tour, or even a ride in a "duck" can be a fun way to learn about a town or city you're visiting. But one of the most interesting, *creepy* ways to get to know a place is through its ghost stories. Every place has them—the older the locale and the more history it has, the more ghosts you'll find there. Even if you don't believe in ghosts, taking a ghost tour is entertaining *and* informative. You'll meet with a guide in the early evening, just as the shadows are starting to look a little spooky. You'll set out, often by the light of a lantern, and hear old tales that have been repeated over and over again through the years, usually containing a bit of truth and a lot of embellishment. Underneath all the gory details, a ghost story preserves part of history and makes us feel connected to people of the past. And you never know: it *could* be true.

27 GIVE YOUR ROOM A MAKEOVER

You've seen the shows on TV—a bus pulls up to a house and a team of experts makes some kid's room into a recreational palace, with a climbing wall, a ceiling embedded with fiber-optic stars, and a tent bed. You may not get a visit from a TV crew, but that doesn't mean your room can't get a new look. You probably spend more time in your room than any place in your house. Even if you share it with a sibling, it should express a little about who you are. Ask your parents whether you can paint (even just one wall) or put up some pictures, posters, or your own artwork. Temporary changes are just as good as permanent ones. Moving the furniture around changes not only the way your room looks but also how you feel about being there. You don't need a team of experts to do it—just your imagination.

28 PLANT SOMETHING AND WATCH IT GROW

This sounds like a really easy thing to do. But if growing something were as easy as putting a seed in the ground (or in a pot) and covering it with dirt, the world would be a much greener place. In reality, a little seed has a lot to overcome in order to grow. Nature is pretty powerful; sun and rain are good things for a plant, but too much of a good thing can be bad. There are all kinds of creatures who want to eat a growing seed: grubs, aphids (called plant lice), voles, and even cute little deer and bunnies. If you want your little seed to grow up, you're going to have to look after it. Make sure it gets the right balance of sunlight and water, and protect it from predators and harsh weather. It'll take some dedication, but when you see your plant blossom and thrive, you'll be proud that you helped make it happen.

GROW YOUR OWN WAY

Here are some ideas for great ways to grow:

MIDNIGHT GARDEN

Plant a glowing moonlit garden, featuring plants with white flowers, silvery leaves, or exotic nighttime fragrances. Plants include moonflower, silver sage, flowering tobacco, and evening scented stock.

PHYSIC(K) GARDEN

If you were a medieval alchemist, you'd have medicinal herbs and plants with healing (and magical?) properties in your garden. Plants include yarrow, chamomile, witch hazel, lemongrass, and thyme.

PERFUME GARDEN

Violets, roses, lavender, lemon verbena, rosemary, and eucalyptus make a fragrant garden. You can dry or crush petals and pods and make them into potpourri.

BUTTERFLY GARDEN

Butterflies love butterfly bushes (of course), butterfly weed, ginger lily, purple coneflower, phlox, and cosmos. Plant them and enjoy your winged visitors.

PIZZA GARDEN

From your garden to the kitchen table—plant oregano, parsley, pepper, basil, and tomatoes (sorry, you can't grow pepperoni).

WATER/BOG GARDEN

If you have a pond or water feature, you can grow water lilies, lotus, and cattails, all frog-friendly plants. For a really moist place that's not quite in the water, try "bog garden" plants, including iris and horsetail; you can even try some carnivorous plants (they eat insects, not people).

CONTAINER GARDEN

Don't have a yard? Plant flowers, herbs, or even vegetables in a container. Plants that like the same conditions (such as sunlight and dry soil) should share the same pot. Get a container that's big enough for your plant and all its roots at its full-grown size, and make sure the container provides drainage at the bottom for excess water.

47

29 Give Shakespeare a Chance

Give the Bard a break. Being called the greatest writer in the history of the English language creates a lot of pressure, a lot of high expectations. When some kids read a little Shakespeare and come across a lot of "thithers" and "thous," they think, "*This* is supposed to be great?" Elizabethan English isn't always easy to understand in writing, but you'll really *get* Shakespeare if you see one of his plays on stage. Ghosts, hideous monsters, backstabbers, and practical jokes—it's all good stuff and it's all there. Even if you don't understand all the words, you'll understand the people and their actions. Try one of the more kid-friendly plays first: *MacBeth*, *The Tempest*, *A Midsummer Night's Dream*, or *Hamlet*. A great Shakespearean play with cool sets and costumes beats any movie you'll see at your local multiplex, hands down. See Shakespeare in the summer at an outdoor theater (see page 127) and you've crossed two items off your gotta-do list.

30 PYO (Pick Your Own)

It's one of the early signs of summer, when you're driving along in the countryside and you start to see signs with the initials PYO. Translation: pick your own _____ (strawberries, tomatoes, peaches, melons, oranges) right from the field or tree at the local farm or orchard. When you see the PYO sign, make your parents pull over; it's worth the stop. Some people say that you've never really tasted a tomato until you've had one warm and fresh from the field, so find out for yourself. The PYO farmer will give you a basket to fill, and you can get whichever ones you like. In late summer and fall, you can pick your own apples from an orchard and even pick your own Halloween pumpkin—it's much more fun than getting one at the supermarket.

Sometimes the best PYOs are found just by driving by. But you can also check www.pickyourown.org to locate one in your area, or do an Internet search for "pick your own" and your state or province.

31 See the View from the Top

However you get there—a stomach-turning elevator ride, a long hike, or a climb up a ton of stairs—the view from the top of something really tall is worth the effort. Whether it's the tallest building in your city (or in the country) or the highest mountain you can find, getting to the top not only gives you bragging rights, but it also gives you a whole new perspective. Gazing down on an urban area, the cars look like beetles and the people look like ants, and you can see how the city spreads out for miles. At high elevations in the mountains, you feel like you're on top of the world—you might even get to walk through a cloud. If you go up high enough, you reach a whole different weather system. If you're acrophobic (afraid of heights), take it easy; there's no need to attempt Mount Everest right away. Start small and work your way up.

32 See an Eclipse

In ancient times, people had some pretty interesting explanations for eclipses. Hindu legend said that demons caused them, and Chinese myth claimed a frog was sitting on top of the sun. Now we know they happen when one celestial body casts a shadow on another. The rarest kind of eclipse is the solar eclipse, when the moon moves in front of the sun from Earth's point of view. Your best bet for seeing one before you're 12 will take place on August 1, 2008 at 10:21 A.M. EST (visible only in the eastern United States, Europe, and Asia). If you happen to be in extreme northern Canada, you'll see a total eclipse; in other place, it will be partial. Your next best chance to see a total solar eclipse will be on August 21, 2017 at 6:25 P.M. EST. It will be the first total solar eclipse visible in most of the United States (Oregon to South Carolina) since 1979. It's more or less a once in a lifetime thing, so don't miss it.

33 EXPLORE A TIDE POOL

There's nothing in the world as vast as the sea, and nothing as mysterious as the creatures that live in it. Usually they're found in the murky depths, too far down for us to see. But when the tide goes out each day, it leaves behind a patchwork of pools scattered across the beach or under the rocks, and in each one you can get a look at the usually hidden life of the sea. A tide pool is a new place twice a day, every day, with new inhabitants and new treasures to discover. Depending on what coast you're on, you might find sea anemones, star fish, hermit crabs, limpits, or even an octopus. Creatures who live in tide pools are, by nature, secretive. If you want to get close to them, be quiet and still—most only show themselves when they think no one's looking. Don't take any living creatures with you, but you can take cast-off shells, sea glass, or other cool tokens the sea offers up to you before the tide rolls back in.

A TALE OF TWO TIDE POOLS

Rocky coast or sandy shore: what kind of animals will you find in a tide pool?

ROCKY SHORE

The rocky shores of the North Atlantic and Pacific coasts provide a hiding place and a home for creatures such as barnacles, mussels, sea stars (starfish), sea anemones, sea urchins, limpets, whelks, and even lobsters.

SANDY SHORE

The coasts along the Gulf of Mexico, the Caribbean Sea, and the southern Atlantic are usually shallower than those on rocky shores. But they still contain interesting animals, including sea stars (starfish), sand dollars, hermit crabs, jellyfish (don't touch!), and shells of all kinds.

34 Watch the Sunrise on the Beach
(or Somewhere Else Dramatic)

Yes, you are going to have to get up really early for this, but it will be worth it—*really*. There is something indescribable about watching the world transition from night to day, from cold and dark to warm and light, and listening to the birds wake up and start singing. In French, this time of day is called *l'heure bleu* ("the blue hour"), because of the unique blue-black color that starts to appear in the sky. In many cultures around the world, it's thought to be a magical time. If you're able to get to an east-facing beach, this time of day is even more amazing. Watching the sun rise slowly out of the water, tinting the water and sky first light pink, then reddish, and finally orange, will make an unforgettable impression on you, and you'll forget all about how sleepy you are.

35 Explore Your Backyard Habitat

To find out how you can certify your backyard as a Backyard Wildlife Habitat, go to www. nwf.org / backyard.

It's a place of amazing diversity, teeming with tons of different types of plant and animal life sharing a small space. Where is this ecological paradise? The Amazon? The rain forest of Costa Rica? It's much closer— it's your own backyard (or local park or natural area). There may not be sloths or piranhas living there, but once you really start to look, you'll probably find dozens of different types of insects, birds, and plants. Map your yard: plot out which plants and animals live where. If your backyard ecosystem isn't as diverse as you'd like, you can add plants that attract birds and butterflies (see opposite page), build a bat house or a hummingbird feeder, or even create a pond where fish, frogs, or turtles will take up residence. You can even make your yard an "official" wildlife habitat. Before you know it, your place will be where all the neighborhood critters want to hang out.

36
Take a Road Trip with a Twist

The next time you take off on a family road trip, why not take a covered wagon instead of the car? Or do a bike tour, with no car involved? You could even go on foot and have a llama carry your stuff for you. There are tons of cool ways to spend your family vacation that don't involve going to a certain magical kingdom/amusement park. You can live out your pirate dreams on a historic clipper ship or see the mighty Mississippi on a paddle wheeler. Or take a theme road trip: do a baseball stadium tour, a volcano tour of the Pacific Northwest, or a leaf-peeping tour of New England. Stay at a farm, a dude ranch, or a lighthouse, and sleep in a tent, a yurt, or an RV. Make your vacation a once-in-a-lifetime (or once before you're 12) adventure.

LLAMA TREK

Hike/camp in the wilderness with a llama by your side to carry your stuff. To find one, do an Internet search with the keywords "llama trek."

LEARNING VACATION

Learn about art, music, sailing, archeology, horseback riding, cooking, or another language or culture through fun activities. To find one, do an Internet search with the keywords "family learning vacations."

"ROOTS" TRIP

Take a trip with your family to the place where your ancestors came from. See whether you can find any information about your family history while you're there.

VOLUNTEER TRIP

Spend your holiday helping out—rebuild a trail in a national park, collect data in the wetlands, or help save sea turtles. To find one, do an Internet search with the keywords "service vacation" or "volunteer vacation."

ECO VACATION

The rain forest, the Everglades, the coral reef, the Arctic—learn about a whole ecosystem by being there. To find one, do an Internet search with the keyword "ecotravel."

COVERED WAGON TRIP

Travel like the pioneers in a covered wagon. Eat your meals from the "chuck wagon" and gather around the campfire at night. To find one, do an Internet search with the keywords "covered wagon tour" or "wagon trek."

CLIPPER SHIP CRUISE

Set sail like the pirates did, on a schooner with tall sails. To find one, do an Internet search with the keywords "family cruise," "schooner," or "clipper ship."

FARM STAY OR DUDE RANCH

What's it like to live on a farm or ranch? Find out on vacation! To find one, do an Internet search with the keywords "agritourism" or "dude ranch vacation."

37 LISTEN TO A STORY

Once you learned how to read for yourself, you probably stopped *listening* to stories. After all, it's one of those things that most kids only do when they're in preschool and going to story hour at the library. But don't write it off so quickly. Listening to a story, especially one told by a great storyteller, is a really different experience than reading one. A storyteller is a cross between an actor and a village elder, the kind of person at whose feet children and grown-ups would gather to learn about history and cultural beliefs. In

listening to a storyteller, you're taking part in a tradition that's as old as the human race, and definitely not just for little kids. Try going to a storytelling festival, where you'll hear tons of stories in one day— funny ones, scary ones, and dramatic ones. And you might pick up some tips on how to be a good storyteller yourself.

To find out about a storytelling festival near you, go to www.sostoryfest.com/ festivals.html.

To learn more about media literacy, go to
http://pbskids.org/dontbuyit
or www.justthink.org.

38 READ YOUR TV

If you watch any TV at all, you see a *lot* of commercials. After you see one, a strange feeling may come over you—you *have* to have that game/toy/breakfast cereal you just saw. You *really, really* want it, right now. You can't get it out of your head. It's almost like you've been hypnotized. In a way, you have been. Advertisers have a lot of ways to get into your head and convince you (or your parents) to buy things. How can you resist the power of these hypnotists? Become media literate. Media literacy teaches you to *read* your TV rather than just watch it so that you can recognize those hidden messages when you see them and figure out what an advertiser is trying to get you to do. It can teach you how to tell advertising fact from fiction, or at least how to think for yourself, so you can make up your own mind.

39 VOTE!

VOTING BOOTH

Voters Register Here!

Just because most people can't vote until they're 18, it doesn't mean you *can't*. On election day all over North America, kids can often cast votes at polling stations (or by mail or online) just like grown-ups, and their votes are counted. They're just not counted *the same way*. Voting is a super-important part of being a citizen of a democracy. If everyone votes, a democracy stays healthy and truly represents the people. But voting tends to be a habit—people do it all the time or not at all—and like many healthy habits, it starts when you're young. If you start voting now, by the time your vote *really* counts, it'll be an easy "good citizen" habit you follow, just like recycling your soda cans and picking up your trash.

For more information on voting and to find a local group, go to www.kidsvotingusa.org or www.studentvote.ca.

40

Express Yourself

Everybody can be creative, each in a unique way. You may be good at "the arts": writing stories, plays, poems, or songs; drawing, painting, or sculpting; dancing, singing, or playing an instrument; or taking photographs, acting, or making jewelry. If so, you can always find a creative way to convey what you're thinking or feeling. But even if you don't consider yourself the artistic type, there are lots of ways to express yourself, such as through cooking, sewing, woodworking, fashion, or even sports. Famous chefs are always known for a certain dish, and you can always tell one pro tennis player or snowboarder from another by his or her unique flair. When you're doing something you really love, no matter what it is, your personal style will come through. Find the thing that makes you happy, and let your enthusiasm shine through.

41 ENTER A CRAZY COMPETITION

KOOKY COMPETITIONS

STRANGE SCULPT-OFFS

International Snow Sculpture Championship
Where: Breckenridge, CO
When: Every January
What: An invitation-only snow-sculpting show that's fun to see www.gobreck.com, search "snow sculpture"

Carnival Ice Sculpture Competition
Where: Quebec City, QC
When: Every February
What: Considered the best ice sculpture competition in the world www.carnaval.qc.ca

Cannon Beach Sandcastle Contest
Where: Cannon Beach, OR
When: Every June
What: Oldest sandcastle contest in the United States www.cannon-beach.net/cbsandcastle.html

Great Sand Sculpture Contest
Where: Long Beach, CA
When: Every summer www.alfredosbeachclub.com/sandcastle.htm

CRAZY FOR CARDBOARD

Milk Carton Derby
Where: Seattle, WA
When: Every July

What: Race in boats made entirely from cardboard milk cartons www.seafair.com/x355.asp

The Great Cardboard Boat Regatta
Where: In several states
When: Mostly summer www.gcbr.com

America's Cardboard Cup Regatta
Where: Crystal Lake, IL
When: Every June
What: Boat race in boats built entirely from cardboard www.cardboardcup.com

RANDOM, RADICAL RACES

International Camel Races
Where: Virginia City, NV

Winning isn't everything, it's fun just to participate. You've probably heard your parents or coaches say this before. It's especially true when you're participating in a really fun competition. Downhill skiing may be amazing, but skiing downhill on a couch is out of this world, even if you're just watching someone do it. Building and launching a boat is a great experience, but when the boat is made of cardboard, and you're racing against others to see who will sink first, it's unforgettable. There are lots of wild and weird competitions that not only challenge your creativity and inventiveness but are also super fun. Are you an awesome sandcastle builder? A champion pillow fighter? A yo-yo master? Do you have really smelly sneakers? There's a competition out there for you. And if you don't want to participate, watching is *almost* as much fun.

CRAZY CONTESTS

When: Every September
www.2camels.com/festival125.php3

Furniture Races
Where: Whitefish, MT
When: Late winter
What: Downhill skiing on furniture
www.blgmtn.com

Kinetic Sculpture Races
Where: Corvallis, OR; Boulder, CO;
Baltimore, MD; Arcata, CA;
Port Townsend, WA
When: Check websites
What: Races in crazy, homemade, wheeled inventions. Search "kinetic sculpture race" for websites

Wayne Chicken Show
Where: Wayne, NE
When: Every summer
What: Contestants act like chickens
www.chickenshow.com

Nathan's Famous Fourth of July International Hot Dog Eating Contest
Where: Brooklyn, NY
When: Every 4th of July
www.nathansfamous.com/nathans/contest

National Odor-Eaters Rotten Sneaker Contest
Where: Montpelier, VT
When: Check website
www.odor-eaters.com/rsc.shtml

Gold Panning Competition
Where: Dalonega, GA
When: Check website
www.dalonega.org

National Yo-Yo Contest
Where: Chico, CA
When: First Saturday in October
www.nationalyoyo.org/contest

World Pillow Fighting Championship
Where: Kenwood, CA
When: Every 4th of July
www.kenwoodpillowfights.com

U.S. Watermelon Seed-Spitting and Seed-Eating Championship
Where: Pardeeville, WI
When: Every September
www.uncommondays.com/states/wi/events/watermelon.htm

Weird Week
Where: Ocean City, NJ
When: Every August
What: All sorts of crazy contests
www.oceancityvacation.com

Make Some Money

There are several ways you, as a kid, can go about getting money:

1. Find it on the ground.
2. Ask your parents for it.
3. Earn it.

The first way takes luck, the second nerve, and the third effort. But despite what you may think, the money you get the third way actually *feels* best because it's really, really *yours*. You may already be getting an allowance or getting some money for helping around the house. But if you want to increase your cash flow (money coming in), you may need to get a little more *entrepreneurial* (creative and business-minded). You could go the classic route and try a lemonade stand, open just a few days in the summer, or you could really go all out and start offering *goods* (things you make yourself) or *services* (like baby-sitting or yard work) on an ongoing basis. Starting and continuing a successful business takes luck, nerve, *and* effort, but it also feels really good.

Getting Down to Business

Here are some business ideas to consider:

GOODS FOR SALE

◆ Food (sell food [such as baked goods or preserves] that you make at a local farmer's market)

◆ Homemade products (candles, soap, beaded jewelry, hair accessories, T-shirts, cards, magnets, accessories you knit, crochet, or sew yourself)

◆ Your own stuff (used books, etc.) at yard sales, at flea markets, or through online auctions

◆ Start a collection, become an expert, and sell to other collectors via the Internet

SERVICES

◆ Babysitting or mother's helper

◆ Yard work (rake leaves, cut grass, water plants, shovel snow)

◆ Pet care (walk dogs, pet-sit for vacationing neighbors, groom or bathe pets)

◆ Elderly assistance (help older neighbors with household maintenance or other chores)

◆ Homework help for younger kids (only pick a subject you're really good at!)

◆ Musical instrument tutoring

◆ Catering help (food prep or cleanup)

◆ Bike repair

◆ Car washing

◆ Newspaper delivery

BUSINESS TIPS

✔ Do something you enjoy—otherwise you might not stick with it.

✔ Make sure you have your parents' permission before you embark on a money-making endeavor.

✔ Give it time—businesses don't grow overnight.

✔ Start small—perfect your business before expanding.

✔ If you need a lot of supplies to make your product, buy them in bulk.

✔ Don't let your job get in the way of homework!

43 Trace Your Roots

For more information on tracing your roots, check out www.rootsweb.com/~wgwkids.

You may secretly hope that, one day, a club-wielding giant with a funny accent will appear at your doorstep to tell you that, in fact, you are *not* just an ordinary kid: you're really a wizard (or witch), and it's time to report to Hogwarts for training. It *could* happen, right? You may not be the long-lost child of an old wizard family, but your *actual* family might be a lot more interesting than you ever thought. Start digging at the roots of your family tree to find out. Family history is more than just names and birthdates. It's the stories handed down from generation to generation; find out whether they're true or exaggerated. It's also family heirlooms, recipes, traditions, and wisdom. Research your family's unique treasures and ways of doing and saying things. All these little pieces add up to a story that might be quite magical in its own way.

Sooner or later, it's going to happen: there's going to be a dance at your school. But even though it's called a *dance*, it ends up being more like a "sit on the sidelines and stare at each other and do anything but" *dance*. Even if you secretly dance up a storm in your room, dancing in front of or *with* other people can be a little uncomfortable at first. That's why it's good to know a few steps or moves that you can count on to use when you need them. There are tons of different dance styles to learn, including swing, ballroom, hip-hop, two-step, salsa, rumba, and the list goes on and on. Find one that you enjoy and practice it (no one's good at it right away). When the time comes and the music is right, you'll be able to step out and have fun without worrying about tripping over your own two feet.

LEARN SOME DANCE MOVES

44

45 EAT A FLOWER
(OR OTHER WILD PLANT)

Lavender flowers—lovely to look at, sensational to smell…
delicious to eat? You may never have thought of the flowers in your
garden as food, but there are actually a lot of edible plants growing wild
all around you. Looking for foods that grow freely in nature is called forag-
ing or wild harvesting, and people have been doing it since prehistoric
times. While you don't want to just go around putting *anything* green in your
mouth (see guidelines on opposite page), you might be surprised at what you
can eat. Dandelions, chamomile, and hibiscus flowers can all be made into tea;
fiddlehead ferns are used in soup; violets and pansies can be candied and used
in desserts. And of course, there are always wild blackberries in the summer, just
waiting to be made into jam or pies. Once you know what's okay to eat and what's
not, look up some recipes and try making a "wild" dinner for your family.

HOW TO EAT A FLOWER

Only eat flowers you're positive are edible (see the list below) and that you're not allergic to. Some flowers are poisonous and can make you very, very sick.

Only eat flowers that you're sure haven't been treated with pesticides—don't eat flowers from florists, garden centers, or the side of the road.

Remove pistils and stamens from flowers before eating—eat only the petals. Clean the flower under cold running water and let it dry on a paper towel.

Pick your flowers in the morning, when their water content is at its highest.

SOME EDIBLE FLOWERS

Anise
Calendula
Chamomile
Dandelions
Fiddlehead ferns
Hibiscus
Honeysuckle
(the berries are
 poisonous—
Do Not Eat!)

Jasmine
Johnny-jump-ups
Lavender
Lemon verbena
Nasturtium
Pansies
Rose petals
Violets

CANDIED FLOWERS

If you like sweet stuff, try making candied violets or rose petals.

With an adult's help, bring 1 cup of sugar and $\frac{1}{3}$ cup of water to a boil in a small saucepan. Drip a little of the syrup into a bowl of cold water. When the drops harden on contact with the water, it means the syrup has boiled long enough.

Remove the pot from the heat and stir. Using tweezers, dip flowers into the syrup. (Be careful—the syrup is hot!) Spread them out on a plate and allow them to dry overnight.

Use candied flowers to decorate a cake or other treat, or serve them with a plate of sugar cookies.

Every city or town has its own mysteries, unsolved murders, unexplained phenomena, or peculiar places that inspire local legends. Be a super sleuth and investigate your own town's puzzling past. A good place to start your investigation is your local library; librarians are actually excellent detectives in disguise. Ask them to help you gather information about your mystery of choice, or if you don't have one in mind, ask whether they can recommend any local legends for you to research. Ask to look through old newspaper articles or local reference guides to search for clues. Go to the mystery spot and check it out for yourself. If none of your local mysteries intrigues you, check out one on a wider scale, such as UFOs, Bigfoot, a famous shipwreck, "magnetic hills," or "spook lights." There are plenty of strange and curious things in the world to investigate. Sometimes, as they say, truth is stranger than fiction.

47 INVENT A NEW GAME OR SPORT

Before there was snowboarding, there was skateboarding, and before that, there was surfing. Each sport grew from the one before, simply because some kids—ones just like you—decided to take something they loved to do, and do it a little bit differently. They changed the rules a little, tried new equipment, or just altered what they had, and eureka!—a new game was born. You're too late to invent broom hockey (ice hockey played with brooms) or disc golf (golf played with Frisbees), but that doesn't mean you can't come up with another new game or sport all on your own, such as a new card game, ball or board sport, swimming pool game, kind of tag, or even a drama game if you're into theater. Play around, twist the rules, and come up with something new. Try an old sport on a new kind of surface or location, or find something new to do with a tennis racquet. Inventing a new game is nothing but fun.

48

HEAR THE CALL OF THE WILD

When you hear a wolf howl on TV, it sounds kind of eerie. When you hear it in person, it'll send a shiver right down to your toes. You hear animal calls every day—dogs barking, cats purring, birds chirping—they're so common, you might not even notice them. But some animals make the most amazing sounds that it's worth going out of your way just to get a listen. During mating season, male elks "bugle," a sound that's so loud it's known to shake the leaves of the trees. The call of the loon (called a yodel, tremolo, whale, or hoot), is so unusual that people even started using the word *loony* to mean "kind of crazy." A peacock's "scream" is surprisingly rude for such a beautiful bird, and if you hear a howler monkey, you'll never forget the sound.

UNUSUAL ANIMAL CALLS

Animal	Call
Alligator	Bellow
Barn Owl	Screech or Shriek
Barred Owl	Hoot
Bittern	Boom
Coyote	Bark
Dolphin	Click
Elk	Bugle
Ferret	Dook
Hawk	Scream
Hyena	Laugh
Loon	Hoot, Tremelo, Wail, Yodel
Moose	Call
Peacock	Scream
Whale	Sing
Wolf	Howl

If you can't hear them in person, try some of these online sites for recordings:

British Library Wildlife Sound Collection
(the largest animal sound library in the world)
www.bl.uk/collections/sound-archive/listentonature/soundstax/groups.html

U.S. Fish & Wildlife Service Sound Collection
www.fws.gov/video/sound.htm

Hedges Hunting and Outdoors:
Montana's Sounds of the Wild
www.hedgesoutdoors.com/sounds.html

The Barn Owl Centre of Gloucestershire
www.barnowl.co.uk/interact/owlsounds/index.asp

Barred Owl (Stratford Landing Elementary School website)
www.fcps.k12.va.us/StratfordLandingES/Ecology/mpages/barred_owl.htm

The Vancouver Aquarium operates Orca FM, the "world's first all-whale radio station." Listen to the live sounds of killer whales or check out prerecorded audio of whale songs at www.spectramedia.net/WhaleLink/orcafm.html.

49 *Make a Movie or Put on a Show*

Putting on a show at home with friends, neighbors, or siblings is a great way to find out whether the acting or directing bug will bite you. First decide on the kind of show you want to do. Will it be an action/adventure movie, a comedy, or a dramatic play? You'll need a script or at least a storyline; write your own or get one from a book. Then there are costumes, props, sound, lighting, and staging to think about. If you're making a movie, you can pick different locations, but for a play you need to decide on a stage (a patio works well, for example). It's a good idea to assign a director to take care of all the details. Hold rehearsals so everyone can practice together (if you're making a movie, you can just do more "takes"). When you're finally ready, gather an audience for your play or host a screening for your movie—it could be your first step on the road to stardom.

Being part of a family isn't always easy. Sometimes you have to do things you don't want to do (like clean your room). But there are times when you wouldn't trade it for the world, like when you're taking part in a family tradition. Traditions are great for holidays or special occasions, but you can develop one around anything. The change of seasons is a great opportunity: make fall leaf-raking more fun with s'mores around a bonfire at the end of the day, or plan a trip to the garden center at the beginning of spring, so each family member can choose something to plant. Make one night of the week family game night or make-dessert night. Or do something together *for others*: bring cookies to your elderly neighbors once a year, or volunteer together at your local soup kitchen. A great family tradition is something that everyone looks forward to doing, so when you propose a new one, make sure everyone likes it, not just you.

50

START A NEW FAMILY TRADITION

Did you know that there are nearly 20 sports represented in the Winter Olympics? And that's just the "small" Olympics. The next Summer Olympics will have events in 26 sports. Think about that when your PE teacher suggests kickball *yet again*. You've probably played it (and soccer and softball and volleyball) about a million times already, but there are so many sports out there that you may have never tried or even heard of: "extreme" sports, like windsurfing and wakeboarding; martial arts, including tae kwon do and kung fu; individual sports, such as cycling; and team sports like ultimate Frisbee. Even if you're not the most athletic type, there are sports you might enjoy if you gave them a chance. Archery and bowling require precision; fencing is elegant and has a great history; synchronized swimming is beautiful to watch and fun to do. No matter which sport you try, you can easily find groups of enthusiasts to play with (check your local newspaper or look online).

51 Try a New Sport

52 Read Your Cereal Box

It doesn't have a gripping plot, fast-paced action, or colorful characters, but your cereal box is still an interesting read. The "Nutrition Facts" chart, usually located on the side of a box or other package, tells the story of your food and what's in it: the good, the bad, and the ugly. Good stuff includes fiber, calcium, protein, vitamins, and minerals; bad stuff includes saturated fats; and the ugly stuff includes trans fats. Just because a food has some of the good stuff doesn't mean it's necessarily good for you. Read carefully—the facts listed might just be for one serving, and the box may contain many servings, meaning you might end up with more bad stuff than you thought. Reading a food label can be surprising, informative, and even scary. But make a habit of it, and after a while, you'll find that foods that are good for you seem to *taste* better, too.

To learn more about how to read food labels, go to http://pbskids.org/itsmylife/body/foodsmarts/article4.html.

53 See a Reenactment

No one has quite perfected a time machine yet, but until someone does, there is another way to get an idea of what things were like in the past. At a reenactment, you'll get an up-close glimpse of history, with authentic sights, sounds, tastes, and—for better or worse—smells. The most common kinds of reenactments are war battles, but there are lots of other kinds. Many reenactments show major historical events, such as the Salem Witch Trials, the Boston Tea Party, the Oklahoma Land Rush, or a roundup on the Chisholm Trail, as well as small, everyday-type scenes from the past, such as frontier fur trade exchanges. You can go even further back if you like, with Viking ship launches or Roman encampments. It's more exciting than reading about history in a book (even if it is sometimes smellier).

Play It Again

Early Times
Reenactments of pre-seventeenth-century European history (various locations)
The Society for Creative Anachronism, Inc.
www.sca.org

Roman Army Reenactments (various locations)
www.romanempire.net/romepage/Links/
roman_reenactment_groups.htm

Colonial North America
Fur Trade Reenactment, Fur Trade Days, Chadron, ND
www.chadron.com/furtradedays.php

American Revolution
Boston Tea Party Reenactment, Boston, MA
www.oldsouthmeetinghouse.org/calendar/

Civil War
Battle of Gettysburg Reenactment,
Gettysburg National Battlefield, Gettysburg, PA
www.gettysburgreenactment.com

Old West
Harn Homestead Land Run Reenactment,
Oklahoma City, OK
www.harnhomestead.com

Chisholm Trail Roundup Festival, Lockhart, TX
(old West cattle roundup reenactment)
www.chisholmtrailroundup.com

Wild West Gunfight Reenactments,
Old Cow Town, Wichita, KS
www.oldcowtown.org

Medicine Lodge Indian Peace Treaty Pageant,
Medicine Lodge, KS
www.peacetreaty.org

Custer's Last Stand Reenactment,
Little Bighorn Days, Hardin, MT
www.custerslaststand.org

Outlaw Jesse James Capture,
Defeat of Jesse James Days, Northfield, MN
www.defeatofjessejamesdays.org

Historical reenactments of all kinds
www.reenactor.net

54 | Develop Your Own "Signature" Dish

Every family has a famous recipe, known to all by the name of the person who made it their own. Aunt Jill's Famous Brownies or Mom's Grasshopper Pie—no family get-together would be complete without it. Isn't it about time you had your own signature dish? Take something you already know how to make, then add your own special flair to the recipe. The trick is to experiment a lot and create just the right combination of flavors. Before you know it, your friends and family will be begging you to make your famous peanut butter sushi or your mouthwatering cream cheese hot dog roll-ups. Your culinary creation may even become such a hit that its fame extends beyond your family and into the world— could you be the namesake of the next eggs Benedict?

WHO WAS ALFREDO?
And Why Is There a Fettuccine Named After Him?

Have you ever wondered who Graham was and why he had a famous cracker named after him? Or why a corned beef sandwich on rye is called a Reuben? Read on to find out!

Fettuccine Alfredo: A cream-based pasta dish (a favorite with those who don't like tomato sauce) named for Alfredo di Lelio, an Italian restaurant owner who invented it in his restaurant in Rome around the turn of the twentieth century.

Bananas Foster: A dessert made with bananas, brown sugar, and rum that's set on fire, then served over vanilla ice cream. It's named for Richard Foster, friend of Owen Brennan, owner a famous New Orleans restaurant where it was first served.

Earl Grey Tea: A black tea flavored with bergamot orange rind, named for Charles Grey, 2nd Earl Grey, Viscount Howick, and British Prime Minister (1830–1834).

Graham Crackers: A whole-wheat flour and honey cracker created by Sylvester Graham, a nineteenth-century American Presbyterian minister and businessman who promoted healthy living.

Melba Toast and Peach Melba: A dry, thin slice of toast and an ice cream and peach dessert, both named for Dame Nellie Melba, a famous Australian opera star who's said to have eaten the toast when she was ill. The dessert was created by a London chef who was a fan of Dame Melba.

Reuben: A grilled corned beef and sauerkraut sandwich, said to have been created either by Arnold Reuben, a New York City restaurant owner, or Reuben Kulakofsky, a Nebraska grocery store owner.

Sandwich: Said to be named after John Montagu, the eighteenth-century 4th Earl of Sandwich. He didn't invent the sandwich, but he ate them so much that his name became synonymous with it.

Crêpes Suzette: A flaming crêpe dessert said to have first been made in a Paris café for Prince Edward VII and named after his girlfriend.

Tootsie Rolls: A chewy candy named for Clara "Tootsie" Hirshfield, the daughter of Leo Hirshfield, a nineteenth-century New York candymaker.

General Tso's Chicken: A Chinese-American dish said to be named after General Tso Tsung-t'ang of the Qing Dynasty.

Eggs Benedict: A dish made with poached eggs, toasted English muffins, bacon or ham, and hollandaise sauce, named after either New York stockbroker Lemuel Benedict or Mr. and/or Mrs. LeGrand Benedict, a wealthy New York couple.

55 GO TO A GRAPE STOMP

For thousands of years, people all over the world have celebrated the grape harvest season in the same way: by taking off their shoes, stepping into a barrel of grapes, and smushing them between their toes. Even though there are faster and more modern ways to crush grapes these days, a grape stomp is a fun tradition that people look forward to every year. There are grape stomps held each year between late summer and early fall in almost every state and province (look in your local paper or do some Internet research to find one near you). At some grape stomps, you'll even be able to participate. Imagine the feeling of thousands of grapes beneath your feet, popping open and turning to mush— it's squishy, squashy fall fun that you'll never forget.

To find a grape stomp near you, do an Internet search with "grape stomp" and the name of your state or province.

56
Swim with Dolphins

Dolphins are quite possibly the world's most adorable creatures. Everything about them—from their sleek motion in the water to their gentle nature to the cute "smiles" on their faces—makes them lovable. Ordinarily, you only get to see a quick glimpse of them as they frolic under the ocean waves, but there are some places where you can actually swim with them, or even rub them on the head. Getting to swim with a dolphin is a special experience, and it's not something that you can do *everywhere*. You might have to save up some money to go, but it will definitely be worth it when the dolphin gives you a "kiss" on the cheek.

To find a place where you can swim with dolphins, do an Internet search using the keywords "dolphin swim" or "swim with dolphins."

57 FLY A KITE

One day, you'll wake up and look out the window to see the wind steadfastly blowing, tossing everything in its path up and about. You may be the first one to think of it, or someone else might beat you to it, but eventually, someone will say, "It's a good day to fly a kite." These days don't come around all the time, so when one does, get a kite, and let it take to the wind. Kite flying is fun, challenging, and completely unpredictable; you never know which way the wind is going to blow, and it can change at a moment's notice. While you're trying to keep your line untangled and your kite out of a tree, you'll also learn a lot about wind currents and aerodynamics (did you know kites were the first airplanes?). Once you've got your kite up in the air, time it to see how long you can keep it there, or challenge a friend to a kite race, and keep it going as long as the wind is blowing.

58

Be a Shadow for a Day

What do you want to be when you grow up? You may already know for sure, or you may have several *very* different ideas (an archeologist or a hockey player). You've still got plenty of time to make up your mind (and change it more than once), but there's a good way to find out what it would *really* be like to do what you *think* you want to do: be a shadow for a day. Shadowing is just like it sounds: you follow someone around watching what she does. Of course you have to let her *know* you're following and why (otherwise, you'll just be annoying), but most grown-ups are happy to share what they know with someone who might want to follow in their footsteps. Check with your teachers or counselors to find out whether your school has a shadowing program, or ask them to help you set up a shadow day.

59 Hike, Ski, or Pedal Hut to Hut

If your idea of roughing it is staying at a hotel with no swimming pool, you might want to skip this one. But if you're up for an adventure, try hiking, skiing, or mountain biking from one hut to another. You start out on a trail (no roads or cars in sight) and hike, ski, or mountain bike (for a few hours to all day) until you reach a "backcountry" hut or lodge. The reward for your effort is an amazing view, rest for your weary legs, a comfy bunk or bed (way more comfy than a tent), and a chance to meet fellow travelers. Some huts will even treat you to a surprisingly delicious meal (at others you make your own). There are trails of all lengths for beginners to experts. Start easy—you can try the harder ones *after* you're 12.

A Good Hike and a Warm Bed

In Europe, you can find hut trails almost anywhere there are mountains, but the tradition is just starting to grow in the United States and Canada. Here are some to try:

ALASKA
Alaska Mountain and Wilderness Huts Association (8 huts above tree line or near glaciers in the Chugach and Talkeetna Mountains)
www.alaskahuts.org

ALBERTA AND B.C.
The Alpine Club of Canada (14 huts in Alberta and B.C.)
www.alpineclubofcanada.ca

CALIFORNIA
Clair Tappaan Lodge (takes reservations for huts in the Donner Pass/Lake Tahoe area)
www.sierraclub.org/outings/lodges/ctl

COLORADO
The 10th Mountain Division Hut Association System (16 huts between Vail and Aspen)
www.huts.org

GEORGIA
Len Foote Hike Inn, Dawsonville
www.hike-inn.com

MONTANA
Sperry Chalet and Granite Park Chalet, Glacier National Park
www.graniteparkchalet.com

NEW HAMPSHIRE
Appalachian Mountain Club's Hut-to-Hut System (10 lodgings in the White Mountains)
www.outdoors.org/lodging/huts

QUEBEC
Gatineau Provincial Park, Chelsea
http://www.canadatrails.ca/hiking/qc/gatineaupark.html

60
Try Letterboxing or Geocaching

A hidden box, a set of clues, a compass. It sounds like the stuff of a mystery book, but it's really the basics you'll need to get started in letterboxing, an adventurous activity that's a bit like treasure hunting. A letterboxer makes his or her own personal stamp, and then puts the stamp, a stamp pad, and a notebook in a waterproof container known as a letterbox. She hides the letterbox—under a rock, in the hollow of a tree, etc.—and then posts clues on the Internet to help others find it. A "hunter" equipped with his own stamp and notebook searches for the box. When he finds it, he stamps each notebook to create a record of the find, and puts the letterbox back for someone else to uncover. Geocaching is a similar "sport" that uses high-tech Global Positioning System (GPS) equipment to locate a hidden "cache" filled with trinkets. Either activity will make you feel like a master detective/pirate/explorer— how can you resist checking them out?

To find out more about letterboxing and geocaching, go to www.letterboxing.org or www.geocaching.com.

Leave Your Mark

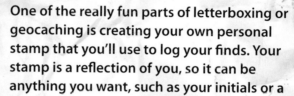

One of the really fun parts of letterboxing or geocaching is creating your own personal stamp that you'll use to log your finds. Your stamp is a reflection of you, so it can be anything you want, such as your initials or a symbol that means something to you (an image of your favorite animal or character, the flower from your birth month, etc.). People often make up a letterboxing name (like an alias) and use it on their stamp.

You can buy a stamp, but you might have more fun carving your own from an eraser.

To read about how to carve your own stamp, go to www.letterboxing.org/kids/kidstamp.htm.

To see some examples of other people's stamps, go to www.ruthannzaroff.com/letterboxing/stamps1.htm or www.ajaster.com/letterboxing/clues.html.

61 FIND THE FIBONACCI

Most people can't even pronounce Fibonacci (fib-o-nah-chee). But once you know what it is, you'll see Fibonacci's sequence everywhere in nature. Fibonacci was a medieval Italian mathematician who discovered a sequence of numbers in which each number equals the sum of the previous two numbers. Here's how the series starts: 1 1 2 3 5 8 13 21 34 55 89 144. You could go on and on, adding the last two numbers to get the next number in the sequence. But what does it have to do with nature? Flowers, leaves, pinecones, shells, and even cauliflower seem to grow according to the sequence. Count the petals on a flower in your yard; you're likely to come up with a number that's part of the sequence. Count the leaves on a stem, the whirls on a pinecone, or the divisions in the spiral of a nautilus shell—you'll find a Fibonacci number. Coincidence? Or evidence that the universe is just one big math problem? You decide.

62 Do a Ropes or Challenge Course

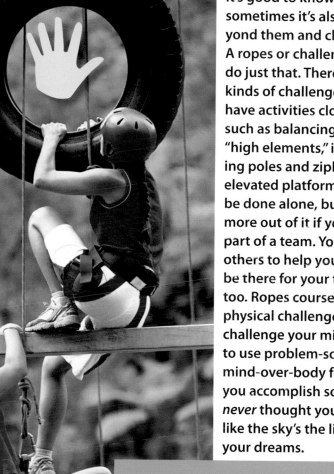

It's good to know your limits—but sometimes it's also good to step beyond them and challenge yourself. A ropes or challenge course lets you do just that. There are all different kinds of challenge courses. Some have activities close to the ground, such as balancing logs; others have "high elements," including climbing poles and ziplines between elevated platforms. A course can be done alone, but you may get more out of it if you participate as part of a team. You'll have to trust others to help you out and learn to be there for your team members, too. Ropes courses are definitely a physical challenge, but they also challenge your mind. You'll need to use problem-solving skills and mind-over-body focus. But once you accomplish something that you *never* thought you could, you'll feel like the sky's the limit for you and your dreams.

Check with your local parks and recreation department to find out where there's a ropes/challenge course near you. Never use a ropes course without a trained instructor present.

START A COLLECTION

WHAT TO COLLECT

Can't decide? Here are some ideas:

Autographs
Books
Bottle caps
Bottles
Coins
Comic Books
Fossils
Lunchboxes
Miniature figures
Photographs
Postcards
Posters
Rocks and minerals
Seashells
Stamps
Teddy bears
Trading cards such as baseball cards

Anyone can *buy* things, but collecting things requires a little more thought, skill, and investigation. A collection is more than just a bunch of stuff—it's a reflection of *you*: what you're interested in and excited about. Whatever you choose to collect, you're really choosing to learn as much as you can about it—to become an expert on the topic. You'll find out what makes your items valuable. Are they rare or hard to find? If so, why? You'll become *discriminating*, not choosing everything, but only the best. You should always choose to collect something because you really like it, not just because you think it might be worth money someday (although that is a nice plus). A collection has value because it means something to *you* and because you put your time and effort into it.

COLLECTING TIPS

Try to get as much information as you can about the objects in your collection: What are they called? What's special about them?

Whatever you collect, its condition is important. Try to collect things that are not broken or too damaged, and then take care of them.

Find a protected place to store and/or display your collection.

Go to yard sales or flea markets where you might find special things at a good price.

Join a club or group for people who collect the same things you do.

Meet or Correspond with Someone Famous

64

Famous people are not like the rest of us—or are they? Chances are that someone you admire—your favorite author, athlete, actor, or musician, for example—was once a kid very much like you, with some of the same dreams you have now. Don't be afraid to write to your hero and explain why you admire him or her. If he or she is scheduled to be in your town, make it a point to get to the appearance. You may be able to get an autograph or be able to see your hero speak, play, or perform in person—it's way better than seeing someone on TV. Don't be disappointed if you can't get any personal contact, though. You'll never forget the time you saw (insert name of president, famous scientist, Olympic champion), even if it was just from the back of a crowd.

YOUR PEN NAME

For your first name: Use the name of your birthstone (girl); Use your name in another language (boy)

For your last name: Use "Le" or "De" plus your mother's maiden name

YOUR SPY NAME

For your first name: Use the name of your first pet

For your last name: Use the name of the street you grew up on (drop the "road," "street," or "avenue")

Or

For your first name: Your favorite color

For your last name: Your favorite animal

65

Make Up a Pen Name or Spy Name

Few people are born with a name as distinctive as Lemony Snicket. And he wasn't born with that name either—it's a *nom de plume*, or pen name. Many famous writers throughout history have adopted pen names for different reasons—so they could write more freely, for example, or because they just didn't like their real names. Women writers, such as George Sand (the pen name of Amandine-Lucile-Aaurore Dupin), wrote under men's names when women writers weren't published. Spies also often change their names to protect their identities; the famous World War I spy Mata Hari was born Margaretha Geertruida Zelle. What would your pen name/spy name be? Use the hints above to make one up.

Host a Party

Hosting a party is even more fun than being a guest at one. You get to decide on the theme, the menu, the decorations, and the games. You don't have to wait until it's your birthday or Halloween to have one, either. Any time of year is a good time for a karaoke gathering or a mystery night. Or you could let the season decide what your party will be. How about a tea or garden party in the spring, a scavenger hunt in the summer, or a skating or sledding party in the winter? You could celebrate a milestone, such as getting your braces off or moving up to a new level in karate, or you could gather friends together for a big event such as the Super Bowl or New Year's Eve. You don't need to have a lot of people for a party; just you and a friend or two is plenty. Whether for two guests or 20, your job as host is to make sure everyone has a good time.

ANY EXCUSE FOR A PARTY

Mad Hatter Party
Ask each guest to bring a hat and supply stuff to decorate it with, such as buttons, feathers, or paint. If you like, make it a tea party, like the Mad Hatter's tea party in *Alice's Adventures in Wonderland*.

Spa Party
Make your own bath and beauty products, and give each other pedicures and facials.

Scavenger Hunt
You make the clues, you hide the prize. Then send your friends out on the hunt.

Backyard Splash Party
Water balloon fights, running through the sprinkler, sliding events, water soakers…

Pumpkin Decorating Party
Supply pumpkins for everyone, plus materials for decorating them such as paint, glitter, and carving tools. (Make sure an adult is close by for any carving activities.)

Dance Party
Pick a kind of dance (salsa, hip-hop, swing, etc.). Provide food, music, and lessons to teach the dance to your friends.

Royal Feast
Ask everyone to dress as royalty and make a medieval banquet at a long table. Look for authentic recipes, and play music from the period.

Fondue Party
Make cheese or chocolate fondue and provide bread or fruit for dipping.

Tasting Party
Make a single kind of food (ice cream, chocolate, cookies, muffins, salsa, etc.) from several different recipes. Invite your friends for a tasting, with everyone picking his or her favorite.

Pizza Making Party
Ask each guest to bring one ingredient, and make the dough beforehand. Assemble and bake your pizzas, and then, of course, eat them together.

67

MAKE YOUR OWN COSTUME

If you buy a standard costume from a store, chances are, on Halloween night you could run into dozens of kids who are dressed just like you—and that could be *really* scary. Halloween is the one night of the year when you can pretend to be someone else, so why wear the same costume as everyone else? Put some thought into what you want to wear and start constructing it early. The more time you have, the more amazing you can make your costume. You could even add special effects, such as battery-operated lights or movable parts. Go all out and make a mask, or paint your face and dye your hair (temporarily, of course). The more effort you put into it, the more fun it will be to wear. And it will probably score you more candy than all those other kids in look-alike costumes.

CREATIVE COSTUME IDEAS

GET A GLOW ON

Create a costume around glow sticks (the kind made into necklaces at carnivals or amusement parks). You could be a glowing alien, a wizard with a magic wand, a firefly, or even a neon sign. Or use glow-in-the-dark paint on white clothes to turn yourself into a skeleton, a ghost, a shimmering mermaid, or an iridescent butterfly.

Use tap or touch lights (found at home improvement stores) on a hat or hood to create giant glowing bug eyes.

BEASTLY CLAWS, PAWS, AND ANTENNAE

Gloves are great for making paws or monster hands. You can glue fake fur onto old gardening gloves, or make spiky talons from egg cartons and hot glue them onto black gloves or mittens. A pair of sunglasses with pipe cleaners attached to the top can become bug eyes and antennae, and you can make a simple beak from craft foam and elastic cord.

WHAT'S AROUND THE HOUSE?

If you've got bubble packing wrap, you can easily wrap yourself in it to be a mummy, hang it from an umbrella and be a jellyfish, or shape it into a snowman costume. Garbage bags? Shred them into a witch costume. Weed cloth in the garage? It's easy to cut into a cape for a vampire or a superhero.

68 HUNT FOR GARGOYLES

Perched on the tops of buildings near you, there are monsters lurking: creatures with wings, horns, and terrifying looks on their faces. Don't worry, though, they're only made of stone: they're gargoyles. During the Middle Ages, gargoyles were carved on churches to serve as waterspouts. Some believed they also kept evil spirits away, coming to life and flying around at night, then turning back into stone at sunrise. Gargoyles have been used in architecture ever since. Sometimes they're creatures, scary or mischievous, and other times they're human faces, or even famous people. In big cities, gargoyle hunting is pretty easy. When you see a Gothic or medieval style– building (think *old*—brick or stone, not modern and glass), look around the eaves, upper windows, and over doorways. Churches and universities are good places to start, but you might even see them on hotels, fountains, gardens, or office buildings. Hunting for gargoyles is fun. When you find one, snap a photo and start your own gargoyle gallery.

GET ON-BOARD

69 Snowboarding, skateboarding, windboarding, surfing—is there no limit to what you can do on a board? No matter what surface you happen to be near, chances are someone has figured out a way to cross it or ride it on a board. You can scoot down a dune on a sandboard, or combine sailing and surfing on a windsurfing board. Or just hop on a friend or neighbor's skateboard and ride it on a flat surface for starters—you may be surprised by how quickly you get the hang of it. You don't have to be a great athlete to give a board sport a try, but in some cases you do need to wear protective equipment, such as helmets or kneepads. There are so many board sports to choose from, you're bound to have fun doing one of them.

You-Won't-Be-Bored Sports to Try

SKATEBOARDING: On wheels on a paved surface

SURFING: On a board, in the water

SNOWBOARDING: On a board, on the snow (of course)

SANDBOARDING: Similar to snowboarding, except on sand

WINDSURFING: Surfing on a special board with a sail attached

KITEBOARDING: Surfing in the water with a kite attached to your board; on a paved surface or on snow, using a board with or without wheels

MOUTAINBOARDING OR DIRTBOARDING: Similar to snowboarding, except with wheels attached to the board and no snow

SOME FAMOUSLY OUTRAGEOUS FESTIVALS

SPAM Museum Jam and SPAMARAMA
(celebrations of SPAM)
Where: Austin, Texas
When: Every summer
www.spam.com or www.hormel.com
www.spamarama.com

UFO Encounter (commemorates supposed
alien crash of 1947)
Where: Roswell, New Mexico
When: Every summer
www.roswellufofestival.com

Loto-Quebec International Fireworks
Competition (amazing fireworks displays)
Where: near Quebec City
When: Every summer
www.lesgrandsfeux.com/en

Chalk Street Painting Festivals
(celebrations of chalk art)
Where: Mission Viejo, Santa Barbara, San
Rafael, and Pasadena, California; Massey,
Ontario; Lake Worth, Florida; Providence,
Rhode Island
When: Check websites
www.youthinarts.org/pages/italian.htm
www.funwithchalk.com
www.imadonnari.com
www.pasadenachalkfestival.com/index.
  php?location=ch_info
www.masseystreetpaintingfestival.com
www.streetpaintingfestivalinc.org/
  Home.htm
www.arts.ri.gov/blogs/index.php/?p=830

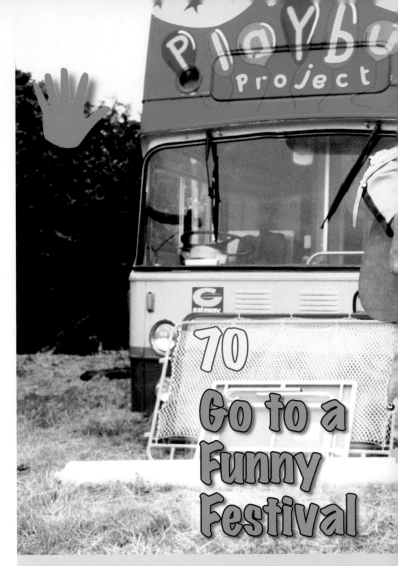

70
Go to a
Funny
Festival

What's so great about canned meat? How big is the world's biggest brownie? How do you drive a coffin? Find out the answers to these and other epic questions at one of the many funny festivals held all over North America. People don't need much of an excuse for merrymaking. Food is a common theme: there are chocolate festivals, crawfish festivals (yes, people eat them), and Spam (canned meat) festivals. Even the

Sylvesta the singing Jester

humble pickle is the focus of a few celebrations. Then there are the festivals that defy easy explanation, such as the UFO Encounter, da Vinci Days, or Emma Crawford Coffin Festival. Some are definitely worth making a special trip for (a kinetic sculpture race must be seen to be believed), but you might find that your very own community hosts a world-class fun festival.

Waterfire ("fire sculptures" on rivers)
Where: Providence, Rhode Island
When: Every summer
www.waterfire.org

da Vinci Days Festival (features da Vinci-like ingenious inventions)
Where: Corvallis, Oregon
When: Every summer
www.davinci-days.org

Pageant of the Masters (live re-creations of famous paintings and sculptures)
Where: Laguna Beach, California
When: Check website
www.foapom.com/

Duncan Hines Festival (featuring "the World's Biggest Brownie")
Where: Bowling Green, Kentucky
When: Every summer
www.duncanhinesfestival.com

Emma Crawford Coffin Festival (races in coffins and other events)
Where: Manitou Springs, Colorado
When: Every Halloween
www.manitousprings.org/coffin_races.htm

Twins Days (gathering of twins)
Where: Twinsburg, Ohio
When: Every August
www.twinsdays.org

Scarecrow Festivals (celebration of scarecrows)
Where: St. Charles, Illionois; Chapel Hill, North Carolina; Edmonton, Alberta; Atlanta, Georgia
When: Every fall
www.scarecrowfest.com

Look through a Microscope or Telescope

What's it like to have a superpower? Try looking through a microscope or telescope. It'll give you a taste of what it's like to have super-vision (like Superman's x-ray vision, but better). A microscope lets you see the nearly invisible—microorganisms that measure less than 4/1000 inch (0.1 millimeter) across. Microscopes can make them look a thousand times bigger, so you get a glimpse into the secret life of bacteria, cells, or tiny organisms that share the world with us. Then there's the telescope, which has a different kind of superpower—it makes faraway objects look closer than they are. The surface of the moon comes into focus with even an ordinary telescope; with a mega-strong one like the kind they have at observatories, you can see into outer space. Find out what amazing discoveries await you beyond the view of the naked eye.

Legends say that when the moon is full, all kinds of strange things happen: people act weird and shape-shifters, like werewolves, take on their animal form. Although studies have proven that nothing especially abnormal happens when there's a full moon, it's still an exciting time to be outside, especially if you're doing something that's usually reserved for the daytime. Without bright light, your other senses are heightened, and you hear and smell things you wouldn't during the day. A hike through the woods or desert, a paddling trip on a lake or lagoon, or a cross-country ski trip on a wide-open field is a totally different experience when you do it by moonlight. Many nature centers, parks, kayak outfitters, and ski clubs offer organized trips that you can join. If you can't find one, ask your parents whether your family can create your own moonlit adventure. (Definitely don't try this one without an adult).

To find a full moon hike, paddle, or ski near you, do an Internet search with "full moon" and the name of the activity you want to try.

72

Stroll (or Hike or Ski or Kayak or...) by the Light of the Full Moon

73 SEE THE LIGHTS

"Luminous phenomena" are lights that seem supernatural but have perfectly scientific explanations. The aurora borealis, also called the northern lights, is one of the most incredible examples. It appears as eerie lights that glow in green, yellow, or blue waves in the upper atmosphere. Seeing it is a once-in-a-lifetime experience, but you'll have to be in the right place at the right time (see opposite page). For another fantastic light show, visit one of the bioluminescent bays in Puerto Rico. On clear nights, millions of dinoflagellates (single-celled organisms) make the water glow. You can swim in it, leaving glowing trails as you move, like swimming in liquid starlight. A little closer to home, you might be able to see what's known as the "green flash" after a sunset. It's a quick flash of green light that appears over the sun just before it dips below the horizon.

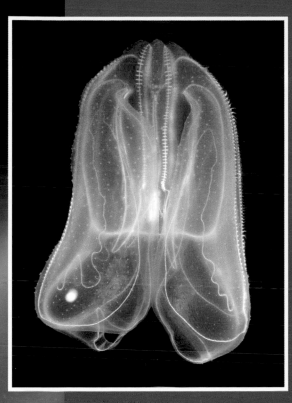

EVERYTHING IS ILLUMINATED

Luminous phenomena and where to find them:

AURORA BOREALIS
WHAT: "Waves" of brilliant-colored light in the upper atmosphere
WHERE to see it: In the United States, Alaska is best, but you can see it sometimes in the northernmost states. In Canada, Yukon, Northwest Territories, and Nunavut are best.
WHEN: March and September

BIOLUMINESCENT DINOFLAGETTES
WHAT: Glowing microorganisms that float in certain bays
WHERE to see them: There are three bioluminescent bays in Puerto Rico
WHEN: On a clear, moonless night

THE GREEN FLASH
WHAT: A flash of green light just as the sun sets below the horizon
WHERE to see it: As you watch the sunset over the ocean or from a high elevation, such as a mountaintop or tall building
WHEN: Just as the sun is about to dip below the horizon
TIP: Don't look directly at the disk of the sun; look just above it.

SPRITES AND ELVES
WHAT: Reddish orange flashes or flickering towers of light above thunderstorms
WHERE to see them: From a distance, with a clear view over a flat horizon (Yucca Ridge in Colorado is said to be the best place in the U.S.)
WHEN: When there's a thunderstorm on the distant horizon
TIP: Look above the storm and don't be distracted by lightning.

74 Somewhere in your home, it's possible that your parents have hours, even days, of video footage of you and your siblings stored away. From your first day on Earth to your first solid food to your first dip in the ocean, the moments of your life were recorded. But does anyone ever watch them? Ask your parents whether you can arrange to have a family film festival—a viewing of all your family's videotapes. Make an event of it and serve popcorn and snacks, turn off the lights, and relive all those happy and embarrassing moments. Even more fun is watching old home movies of your parents when they were kids. Ask your grandparents whether they have any around. If your family doesn't have any film or videos, you can still make a night of taking out all the old photo albums and passing them around. You'll laugh at how you or your parents used to look, remember things you thought you'd forgotten, and just enjoy being part of your family.

Have a Family Film Festival

You can buy astronaut ice cream, space chicken dinner, and space strawberries at www.thespacestore.com/spacefood.html or "space food sticks" at www.funkyfood-shop.com.

Some say that there will be human colonies on Mars and the moon within your lifetime. If that's the case, you'd better start getting used to space food. Eating like an astronaut is not so bad. There are no refrigerators in space, but space shuttle and space station astronauts have more than 250 foods and beverages to choose from in orbit. Meat, cereal, vegetables, fruit, and even macaroni and cheese are available. They're just space processed—freeze-dried, thermostabilized, and packed in pouches. Some space food is identical to camping food (granola bars, nuts, trail mix), and you can find it in your own kitchen. (Peanut butter and jelly wrapped in a tortilla is a space favorite because there are no crumbs to float around and gum up the equipment.) Celebrate the next visit to space with a meal in the astronauts' honor.

To find out more about space food, go to http://spaceflight.nasa.gov/living/spacefood.

76 INTERVIEW AN ELDER

In many cultures without a written language, traditions and stories are passed from generation to generation in just one way: through elders talking and young people listening. These days, we often forget that this age-old way of transferring knowledge is still one of the best. You could read about World War II in a book or the Great Depression in a book, but talking to someone who lived through it is a lot more interesting. Each person has a unique point of view and a story worth telling. Find a topic you're interested in and an older person you'd like to talk to—a grandparent, a neighbor, or someone at a local senior center, for example. Ask your interviewee if you can tape record or write down your conversation. Older people also provide a link even further into the past: they can tell you about *their* parents' experiences, spanning back into another century—find out how far back in time you can reach with just a few questions.

SOME SAMPLE QUESTIONS

- Did you know your grandparents or great-grandparents? What do you remember about them? Did you ever hear them talk about their lives?

- How is the world now different from what it was like when you were a child?

- Do you remember someone saying something to you that had a big impact on how you lived your life? What was it?

- What was the happiest time of your life? The scariest?

- Is there anything you have always wanted to do, but haven't?

ORAL HISTORY HOW-TOS

Look for people who want to talk to you about their experiences. Try veterans' organizations and senior citizens' centers, and ask the director whether there's anyone who'd like to talk to you.

Do some research first. Find out about events that took place during your interviewee's lifetime and ask how he or she experienced those events.

Prepare some questions in advance to help get the ball rolling. Follow your list of questions, but don't be afraid to ask others.

Use a tape recorder and/or take some notes as you listen so you don't forget the answers.

You probably do a lot of things to keep your body sharp, strong, and healthy, but what about your mind? It can get a little flabby, too, if you don't exercise it. Fortunately, there are a lot of ways (other than home-work) to do that, and some of them are really fun. From crossword puzzles (try completely finishing a challeng-ing one without cheating) to board games to classic games of strategy like checkers and chess, there are lots of ways to give your brain a workout. There are games you can play by yourself and games you play with others, and each has its own unique challenges. Try to make a point of giving your brain a workout at least once a week—if you keep it in good shape, it will last a lifetime.

GAMES OF SKILL & STRATEGY

Backgammon
Checkers
Chess
Chinese Checkers
Go
Monopoly
Pente
Rummikub
Tournament Scrabble
Stratego
Bridge
Suduko puzzles
Othello
Logic puzzles
Mastermind

78 GO CLIMBING

You've probably been climbing ever since you could crawl: up onto chairs, out of your bed, and later into trees. Now it's time to really challenge yourself. Try a climbing wall or the real thing: rock climbing. It's not easy, and it shouldn't be tried without an experienced adult there to show you how. But when you've got the right equipment, the right training, and most of all, a spirit of adventure, it's an amazing experience. You'll be suited up with a harness and ropes for safety, and once you're on your way, there's nowhere to go but up. You might have moments of doubt along the way (don't look down!), but keep going. There's nothing like the feeling of getting yourself to the top of something you never thought you could reach.

You're soaring over your neighborhood, flapping your arms like wings. You're freefalling through a canyon, faster and faster, until suddenly—you wake up. Everyone has dreams: some happy, some scary, and some just really weird. You spend almost one-third of your life asleep, and that's a lot of time to dream. Even if you don't always remember your dreams, you have dreams four or five times a night. Dreams are a key to unlocking the secrets of the subconscious mind, that mysterious part of your brain where you keep thoughts and feelings that you're not really aware of. There are certain symbols or actions in dreams (such as falling, flying, and running) that are said to have universal meaning. That is, many people have dreams with these symbols or activities, and experts say they represent certain emotions. Other images in your dreams might just be memories or thoughts of you and your life. Or images might be your subconscious mind saying things while you're asleep. Try keeping a dream journal or log (see opposite page). Can you find hidden meaning in your dreams?

KEEP A SLOG

Want to try to understand your dreams? A sleep log, or "slog" is a place where you keep a record of your dreams. Try to write down as many details as you can about your dreams soon after you wake up. See whether there are events or people who show up in your dreams frequently—they may be a clue to figuring out what your subconscious is trying to tell you.

What Does It Mean?

Everyone's dreams are different, but some researchers believe that there are "universal symbols" that mean the same thing no matter whose dream they show up in. Here are some of the common activities that happen in dreams, and what some scientists think they mean.

Being chased: You are facing a challenge or pressures in your waking life and are trying to figure out how to "escape" it.

Climbing: You are close to coming to a solution to a problem.

Falling: You are worried about something and don't know what to do about it.

Flying: You feel free and have overcome a problem.

Floating: You feel free, happy.

Did you know that over a lifetime, the average person sleeps for 233,600 hours—that's more than 26 years!

80 Celebrate April Fools' Day

There's one, and only one, day of the year when it's not only okay to play tricks on people—it's expected. April Fools' Day is said to have started in the sixteenth century, when the calendar changed and New Year's Day was moved from April 1 to January 1. Some people continued to celebrate New Year's Day on April 1, and others made fun of them, calling them "April fools." Nowadays, it's celebrated with pranks, *harmless pranks*—they're funny, not mean; no one gets hurt, and even the person who gets "pranked" can laugh about it. A lot of pranks have to do with food—switching sugar and salt, or offering someone a cookie made with onions. Then there's the simple joke of asking someone whether he did his homework when there really wasn't any, or putting something surprising (like fake bugs) in a friend's lunch bag. Come up with the perfect prank for a friend, but stay on your toes—somebody just might be planning a surprise for *you*.

81 BREATHE UNDERWATER

You don't have to have gills (or superpowers) to breathe underwater, but you do need a snorkel. It's a funny word, but a snorkel is a great invention that lets you get a closer look at the amazing world under the sea. Add a face mask and fins, and you're ready to become an underwater explorer. For your first try at snorkeling, practice in a pool (or even in your bathtub!). Make sure your mask fits well—tight enough to prevent water leaks, but not uncomfortably tight (the same applies to your fins). Fit the snorkel in your mouth and practice breathing through it. When you've got the hang of it, first try snorkeling in calm, shallow water (always with a parent or an instructor nearby). You can snorkel in lakes or rivers, if the water is warm enough, but the ocean is the place for the ultimate snorkeling experience. Swimming side by side with fish, squid, turtles, or an octopus, or exploring a coral reef, is an experience you'll never forget.

82 | *Have a Close Encounter with a Wild Animal (kind of)*

We share this planet with a lot of fascinating animals, some of whom we only read about or see on TV. Some we get to see in person, but only at a zoo or an animal park, where they can't completely be themselves. But seeing a wild animal in its natural habitat is a completely different experience. You can watch them as they do what they naturally do, whether it's searching for food, sending out a mating call, or taking a bath. While you're watching though, keep your distance and give the animal respect. When you're in the wild, you're a guest in the animal's home and you need to follow the rules (a slip-up could be dangerous, or even fatal). Go with an expert or a professional guide who can teach you a lot about animal behavior (see opposite page for some wild-watching ideas), and bring your binoculars so you can get a good look without getting too close.

Where the Wild Things Are

Here are some good spots for wild-animal watching:

Moose

Cape Breton Highlands National Park,
    Ingonish Beach, NS
Moosehead Lake, ME
"Moose Alley," from Pittsburgh, NH,
    to the Canadian border
Algonquin Provincial Park, near Whitney, ON
Isle Royale National Park, Houghton, MI
Ham Lake, MN
Glacier National Park, West Glacier, MT
Antelope Flats, Yellowstone National Park,
    near Gardiner, WY
Moose Valley Provincial Park,
    near 100 Mile House, BC
Denali National Park, Denali Park, AK

Bears

Churchill, MB (polar bears)
Yosemite National Park, CA (black bears)
Quesnal Lake, BC (grizzly bears)
Katmai National Park, AK (brown bears)

Whales

Witless Bay, NF (humpback, fin, pilot whales)
Bay of Fundy, NB (humpback, fin, minke
    whales)
Provincetown or Plymouth, MA (North
    Atlantic right, humpback, fin whales)
Monterey, CA (humpback, gray, blue,
    minke, orca whales)
Gold Beach, OR (gray whales)
San Juan Islands, WA (orca whales)
Vancouver Island, BC (humpback, gray,
    orca whales)
Maui, HI (humpback whales)

Wolves

Lakota Wolf Preserve, near Hainsburg, NJ
St. Vincent National Wildlife Preserve,
    near Apalachicola, FL (red wolves)
International Wolf Center, Ely, MN
Yellowstone National Park, near
    Gardiner, WY
Denali National Park,
    Denali Park, AK
Sonoran Desert Museum, Tucson, AZ
Wolf Mountain Sanctuary,
    Lucerne Valley, CA

What on earth does *carbon neutral* mean? Here's the basic idea: carbon dioxide (CO_2) is what's called a "greenhouse gas"—a harmful gas released by burning fossil fuels such as oil, coal, and gas. Every time you turn on a TV or ride in a car, energy is consumed, and carbon dioxide is released into the air. When you think about how much energy you use every day, and multiply that by all the millions of others doing the same, it adds up to a lot of damage to the atmosphere. Try being carbon neutral, or cutting down on your "personal emissions." Walk or bike somewhere instead of having someone drive you, use fluorescent lightbulbs, and unplug appliances you're not using. Plant trees—they absorb carbon dioxide—and recycle as much as you can. Even little actions can go a long way to help Earth's atmosphere.

83
GO CARBON NEUTRAL

To get an idea about how much carbon dioxide you create each day, visit www.carboncounter.org.

To be part of the postcard project, go to http://postcrossing.com. For a different kind of international Internet exchange, check out www.toyvoyagers.com (a tracking game for toys that travel around the world).

84 See the World without Leaving Home

Here's a way to get faraway places delivered to your mailbox. With your parents' permission, you can sign up online for postcards from around the world. Just make up an ID (not your real name) for yourself, and you'll receive addresses to send a postcard. On the postcard, you can write whatever you like: give information about your part of the world, or ask questions for the postcard receiver to answer. Sign the postcard with your ID, and then send it. Wait a while and, for each postcard you send, you'll get back two postcards from somewhere in the world. You'll never know where the postcards are coming from, so you'll always have a great surprise in the mail.

85 MAKE EDIBLE ART

You might not have ever thought of your refrigerator as an art-supply cabinet, but it contains plenty of stuff for making art *and* making meals. Food sculpture is a little-known art form that's tons of fun and easy enough for anyone to do. Anything round (grapefruit, oranges, tomatoes) can be a head, and anything fluffy or bushy (parsley, broccoli, dill) can be hair. Celery sticks make great legs; beans, peas, raisins, and olives can become eyes; and string beans look like tails. Try making a carrot-stick person with radish legs, raisin eyes, and cilantro hair. Peanut butter and cream cheese are great "glue" for holding everything together. Or use toothpicks and marshmallows to create various creatures. Use your imagination and come up with your own amazing food art. Better still, have an edible art party with your friends, and eat your creations when you're done. (Make sure you take pictures first!)

You probably know how to do a lot of things that kids 100 years ago could never have imagined doing, such as use a computer, a digital camera, and a cell phone. But believe it or not, kids back then probably knew how to do things that you don't. They could whip up a batch of soap or a bundle of candles, make paper, books, or even sew their entire wardrobe. You could just buy all those things, but since you don't *have to* make them, doing it is pretty fun. It'll be easier for you than it was back then, because you can get most of what you need at a craft store, and you've got tools and machines to help. Try making something that you'll use yourself or that you can give as a gift, such as soap or shampoo, a tie-dyed T-shirt, or a birdhouse. Try different crafts or specialize in one. You might even be able to make it into a business (see page 65).

What's a fossil? It's something left behind by a plant or an animal that once lived on Earth—ancient teeth, bones, shells, and footprints; leaves and seeds; and "impressions" left by prehistoric creatures, or even an entire creature. The artifact became trapped in sediment that hardened around it, preserving it for thousands or even millions of years. The cool thing about fossils is, you don't have to be an archeologist to find one—kids find them all the time. The key is to look in the right places—basically, anywhere there's very old exposed sedimentary rock. An old rock quarry or a rocky seashore are places to start. Check with your science teacher or local natural history museum to find out where you might find fossils in your area. Even if you don't find one, digging for them is fun. And if you do find one, you'll have a piece of ancient history to keep.

FOSSILS TO FIND

There are tons of different fossils, but here are some of the most common ones you might find:

PLANTS: ferns, ancient tree bark, leaves
SHELLFISH: coral, clams, snails, seashells
TRILOBITES: bug-like animals
STROMATOLITES: single-celled organisms
BONES AND TEETH: from dinosaurs, fish, mammals
TRACE FOSSILS: footprints, nests, bite marks

For more information on finding and identifying fossils, check out:

www.sdnhm.org/fieldguide/fossils
www.colossal-fossil-site.com
www.backyardnature.net/g/fossils.htm

Although you can find fossils anywhere, some of the biggest fossil finds in North America have been made here:

Florissant Fossil Beds, Florissant, CO
www.nps.gov/flfo

Agate Fossil Beds, National Monument, Harrison, NE
www.nps.gov/agfo

Hagerman Fossil Beds National Monument, Hagerman, ID
www.nps.gov/hafo

John Day Fossil Beds National Park, Kimberley, OR
www.nps.gov/joda

McAbee Fossil Beds, Cache Creek, BC
www.dll-fossils.com

88 THANK A TEACHER

There's a famous bumper sticker that says "If you can read this, thank a teacher." Even if you are one of those kid geniuses who taught *yourself* to read when you were three, the bumper sticker makes a good point. Kids and teachers have a famously tricky relationship. You are required to be together almost every day, sometimes year after year. There are times when you're both actually having a good time, and others when neither one of you wants to be at school. When you go through so much with one person, it's easy to take him or her for granted—you know, not really appreciate them. That's why it's good to remind yourself to say thanks, even just once. You can write a thank-you note (your teacher will keep it forever) or you can just pick a moment and say thank you and mention something you appreciate—a little thank you goes a long way.

89 See an Outdoor Play or Concert

Seeing a play or concert anywhere is cool, but there's something really exciting and different about seeing one outdoors. The sky is the ceiling, the trees are the walls, and the sun and the wind provide lighting and special effects. Your seat might be a blanket in the grass, so you can spread out (great if you're the squirm-in-your-seat type) and maybe even eat as you watch or listen. You feel closer to the performers than you do in a theater, and that makes everything feel a little more real and a little more dramatic. Outdoor performances almost always happen in late afternoon or early evening in the summer (the best time of year to be outdoors). As the sun goes down, candles start to flicker, and the atmosphere takes on a magical quality. Anything can happen, and on stage it just might.

90 Be a Tourist in Your Own Town for a Day

What's cool about the place where you live? Probably a lot more than you think. But most of the time, all you see is the same old places: your neighborhood, your school, the local park. One day, try seeing your town as a tourist would see it. Stop by your local tourist office or chamber of commerce and pick up some brochures to plan a day of sightseeing. Grab a map and your camera, and set out to explore. Ride the bus or subway instead of being driven in a car, or take a super-touristy tour such as a carriage, trolley, or rickshaw ride to get around. Eat at a touristy restaurant and check out the gift store to see what kinds of souvenirs people buy when they come to your area. Chances are you'll learn things you never knew about your hometown and meet interesting people from all different places, and you'll still get to sleep in your own bed at night.

To find out more about how much interest you earn when you save, use the Compound Interest Calculator 1 at www.coolmath.com/calculators/index.html.

Whether through earning it (see page 64) or a birthday windfall, you find yourself with some money. You might want to take that stash of cash and buy all those new games you've had your eye on. But hold on a second. There's a way you can get even *more* money—by saving instead of spending, thanks to a little thing called compound interest. Compound interest means that your money earns money on its own when it's in a bank or invested in another way. If you're 10 and you invest $100, by the time you're 21, you'll most likely have more than $300. That's $200 extra, all for doing nothing but being patient. If you add to your $100 over the years, you'll have even more. Try putting a little money away now (forget you even have it) and relax; your money will do the work for you.

92 Stop and Smell the (Stinky) Flowers

When you see a flower, one of the first things you might do is hold it to your nose and take in a deep breath. If you happened to do that with a carrion flower, you'd be in for a big surprise: instead of a sweet smell, you'd be inhaling the odor of rotten eggs, dead animals, or a garbage dump. While most flowers emit a sweet smell that attracts insects to help them pollinate, carrion flowers attract bugs that like to eat (as scientists put it) "decaying organic manner"—in other words, dead stuff. Carrion flowers, such as the corpse flower, have some of the biggest, showiest blossoms on the planet, and they rarely bloom, so seeing (and smelling) them is a rare event that you can witness at a botanical garden. Carrion flowers can also be grown at home (preferably outside, where you don't have to smell them all the time).

Corpse Flower

FAMOUSLY STINKY FLOWERS

Check with local botanical gardens to see whether they have any stinky flowers in their collections.

CORPSE FLOWER. This Indonesian flower can be found in some botanical gardens. It grows up to 6 feet tall and blooms only once every one to three years. The corpse flower smells like rotten fish or a rotting pumpkin.

STINKING CORPSE LILY OR RAFFLESSIA: The world's largest flower, it can grow to 3 feet in diameter and weigh as much as 15 pounds. It has a warty texture and smells like a dead animal that's been left in the sun.

LANTERN STINKHORN: A wild-growing mushroom that's said to smell like dog droppings, this plant is considered a delicacy in China.

STARFISH FLOWER: A succulent plant you can grow at home, and its starfish flower emits a smell like rotten gym shoes when touched.

SKUNK CABBAGE: This grows in the wild and smells like the animal for which it's named.

DEAD-HORSE ARUM: This plant lures blowflies into a fly trap with a smell that's so unpleasantly strong it's said to make people pass out.

PLACES TO SEE (AND SMELL) CORPSE FLOWERS IN NORTH AMERICA

San Francisco Conservatory of Flowers, San Francisco, CA

University of Wisconsin-Madison, Madison, WI

Myriad Botanical Gardens, Oklahoma City, OK

The Botanic Garden of Smith College, Northampton, MA

United States Botanic Garden, Washington, DC

Fullerton Arboretum, California State University, Fullerton, CA

Brooklyn Botanic Garden, Brooklyn, NY

Virginia Tech Biological Sciences Greenhouse, Blacksburg, VA

Skunk cabbage

Teach a Little Kid Something You Know

93

If you have a little brother or sister (or even if you don't), you may think that little kids are kind of annoying—they always follow you around and try to do what you're doing. Your parents probably always tell you it's because they look up to you, and it's true. You know a lot of stuff that they don't know yet, and they think you're really cool. One way to get little kids off your back and also be a nice person is to teach them how to do something you know how to do, such as kick a ball, ride a bike, braid hair, or play a game. It's all about your attitude. If you do it willingly, even enthusiastically, you might have fun. You'll feel really good when your little protégé learns something from you and gets it right. It means you're not only a nice person, but also a good teacher (add that to your ever-growing list of wonderful qualities).

For volunteer opportunities in your community (or around the world), check out the postings at www.idealist.org. There are lots of listings for kids!

94 Make the World a Better Place

This may seem like a tall order, especially for someone who's not yet 12. But actually, it's very, very easy to do, and there are so many ways you can do it. Give your time, as a volunteer, to the organization of your choice. You can help people, animals, your neighborhood, your school, or the environment. Help raise money for a good cause, or spread awareness of a problem in the world or in your community by writing about it for your school newspaper or just by telling people about it. Give away some of your things to people who need them more than you do. Visit someone who's sick or lonely. Or simply choose to be nice instead of mean—a little kindness can go a long way toward making the world a better place.

SAVE A PART OF ONE SEASON INTO THE NEXT

Sad to see summer go? You can keep it alive by picking and preserving fruits or vegetables to eat in the fall or winter (see opposite page). Your favorite spring and summer flowers can be pressed and saved, as well. Place a piece of thick paper on a wooden board and your flowers on the paper. Put another board on top and clamp the two together for a few weeks. If you don't have boards and clamps, just put the paper and flowers under a stack of heavy books. The most beautiful fall leaves are worth saving, too. To keep a leaf from turning brown and crumbling, place it between two pieces of wax paper, cover the paper with a towel, and run a warm iron over the towel. That will seal the leaf inside the paper. Then cut around the leaf. If winter's your season, make a snowball or two and save them in your freezer to take out and toss on a steamy summer day.

CAN IT!

Pick fresh raspberries, blueberries, or strawberries (from your yard, a pick-your-own farm or berry patch) in the summer, then make your own jam and enjoy it all winter. Better still, make a big batch of jam and give it away as a gift to friends. All kinds of fruits and vegetables can be preserved as jams, jellies, or relishes (check out a canning cookbook for more information and recipes). Here's an easy recipe to try (get an adult to help).

BERRYLICIOUS JAM

8 four-pint canning jars with lids (available at craft stores, some grocery stores, or online)
1 quart strawberries
1 quart red raspberries
1 pint blackberries
$\frac{1}{2}$ teaspoon butter or margarine
7 cups sugar
1 three-ounce pouch liquid fruit pectin (available at grocery stores or online)

1. Wash the jars and prepare the lids according to the manufacturer's instructions.
2. Wash, chop, and crush the strawberries, getting rid of any stems. When crushed, the strawberries should measure 2 cups. Wash and crush the raspberries to make 1 cup. Wash and crush the blackberries to make 1 cup.
3. Over medium heat, melt the butter in a stockpot and stir in the sugar, and then fold in the fruit. Turn the heat to high. Stir constantly, bringing the mixture to a full rolling boil (a boil that continues even when stirred). Stir in the pectin and boil for 1 minute, stirring constantly. Remove the pot from the heat. Skim off any foam with a metal spoon.
4. Transfer the jam into each jar, leaving $\frac{1}{4}$-inch of empty space at the top. Wipe the jar rims with a clean cloth and attach the lids.
5. Turn the jars upside down to create a good seal. After an hour, turn the jars right side up and press down on the center of the lids (the lids should pull inward and not pop out in the center when pressed). If any lids pop out, turn the jars over and test them again in an hour. Jars with a good seal can be stored on the shelf, while others should be stored in the refrigerator.

If you've ever been the new kid in town or school, you know how hard it can be. Everyone seems to have friends already—you're on the outside, and it's not a great place to be. Even if you've never moved or had to start over somewhere, you can probably remember the first day at a new class or activity. Any new beginning can be uncomfortable at first. What makes things instantly better is when someone says "hi," asks you a question about yourself, or invites you to join in. Be that person who makes the first move, at least once. It could be the start of a great friendship, or it could just be good for your karma (meaning someone will do it for you someday). Either way, you've got nothing to lose, and you'll make somebody's day.

96 Welcome a Newcomer

97 MAKE YOUR OWN KIND OF MUSIC

One of the really cool things about music is that there is really something for *everybody*. You might like to listen to classical, country, folk, hip-hop, pop, world music, or a little of everything. The other cool thing about music is that anybody can make it. Some instruments, such as the piano, violin, or guitar, take a lot of time and practice to master, but it's worth it the first time you play a piece of music that sounds really good. Play by yourself, or start a band, even if you just perform for your family. If you're not sure you want to commit to learning how to read music or taking lessons, try playing around with something a little simpler. Just about anyone can pick up a beat with a tambourine, maracas, or a drum. And then there's the instrument that everyone has: a voice. Sing on your own or along with a tape or CD. Don't worry about how you sound—just have fun.

Imagine you're at a party. Everyone is sitting around quietly, looking bored and uncomfortable. No one can think of anything to do. All of a sudden, it comes to you. "Charades, anyone?" you say, and save the day. Knowing a few party games always comes in handy for those moments when a party or get-together needs a pick-me-up. Party games don't require any special equipment (except possibly a few pieces of paper and a pencil), and the rules are usually pretty simple, so you can remember them in your head and easily explain them to others. Try out the game at home with your family, so that you'll become familiar with the rules and get a little experience before you suggest the game to others. Once you've got it down, you'll always be able to bring a party back from the brink of boredom.

LIFE-OF-THE-PARTY GAMES

CHARADES
The group breaks into teams. One player from each team acts out a word or phrase, such as the title of a book, movie, TV show, or song so that the other players can guess— no words can be used, only gestures (ask your parents to show you the accepted gestures, or look online).

CELEBRITY
Each player gets five or so slips of paper, and writes the name of a famous person on each (the people or characters must be ones that everyone will know). All the slips of paper are put into a hat, bowl, or something else

that can be passed around. The group breaks into teams of two or more, one of which is chosen to go first. The 'clue giver' on each team picks a name from the hat and gives clues to the members of his or her team to try to help them guess the name on the paper. The clue giver is given one minute; if the team doesn't guess, he or she must move on and pick another piece of paper. Names that aren't guessed are put into the hat for another round. Whichever team guesses the most names, wins.

FICTIONARY

For this game, you'll need a dictionary, pieces of paper, and a pen or pencil. One person looks in the dictionary for a word that he/she thinks no one else will know, then announces the word. Everyone writes down a fake definition for the word and gives the definition to the word picker. The word picker announces all the fake definitions, plus the real one. Whoever guesses the correct definition gets a point. The game continues as everyone gets a turn to be the word picker.

STUPID NINJA GAME

This game is better with more players. Everyone stands in a circle. Each person thinks up a "stupid ninja move"—a silly movement with a silly name, such as "dragon chop" or "secret agent." The first player does his or her move, and then the next person must repeat the name plus the move, and add his or her own move. Each player must say the correct name and perform each move, in the correct order, or be eliminated.

99 VISIT A SPLASH PAD OR SPRAYGROUND

To find a splash pad or sprayground near you, contact your town or city parks department, or do an Internet search for: "splash pad," "sprayground," "spray park," or "spray playground" and the name of your area.

On a summer day in the city, when it's hot enough to fry an egg on the sidewalk, a jump into the nearest fountain is tempting. Unfortunately, it's probably against the law. To stay cool and avoid the police, find a splash pad or sprayground instead. Smaller than a massive water park, less crowded than a pool, and usually free, a splash pad is perfect for a quick douse or dunk in the water. While each has a different design, splash pads usually feature devices that cool you off and get you wet: nozzles that spray water up or down; wading fountains; "pipe," "tree," or "mushroom" showers; or mist dispensers. They're often motion- or time-activated, so they can turn on suddenly and take you by surprise. You can plan a trip to a sprayground and bring your suit, or just run through in your clothes.

100 STAY UP TILL MIDNIGHT ON NEW YEAR'S EVE

A new year only comes around once every 365 days, so it's worth losing a few hours of sleep to greet it as it arrives. To toast the New Year, make smoothies or sparkling cider drinks. Count down to midnight as loudly as you can. When the clock strikes 12, bang kitchen pots and pans together outside, or shake maracas and blow noisemakers. Make your own confetti drop: put tons of confetti on top of a tablecloth, and secure the cloth to the ceiling with tape or thumbtacks. Then yank it down at midnight. Or, for the same effect, fill balloons with confetti, blow them up, and burst them at midnight. If your parents (and the laws of your state or province) allow it, light sparklers outside, or just scan the sky for fireworks displays. Once the celebrating winds down, don't forget to talk about your New Year's resolutions with your family or friends. Then sleep late the next day and start the new year refreshed.

101
Make a List of Things to Do for the Next 12 Years

Life certainly doesn't end at age 12. In fact, many would say that some of the most exciting adventures await you in your teens and twenties. You'll go to high school, be eligible to drive, go to college, or start a career. You'll become a "young adult." The future is wide open, and you really can make it whatever you want it to be. Of course, that can be a little overwhelming. With a whole world of possibilities, how do you narrow it down? Make a list (like the one in this book, except it can be any length you want). Include your goals and dreams, and think big! Having a list will help you focus and remember what it is you want to do. Keep your list somewhere safe and check back every once in a while to gauge your progress. You may want to cross some things off your list and add new ones as time goes by—it's your list and your life, so go for it!

PHOTO CREDITS